JANUARY 50 COLORING PAGES FOR OLDER KIDS RELAXATION

SHIH CHIEN HUA

PUBLISHED BY:
SHIH CHIEN HUA
Copyright © 2018

SEABIRD SHOP >50FOR

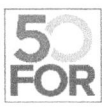

FB FAN PAGE

Disclaimer
The information contained in this book is for general information purposes only. The information is provided by the authors and while we endeavor to keep the information up to date and correct, we make no representations or warranties of any kind, express or implied, about the completeness, accuracy, reliability, suitability or availability with respect to the book or the information, products, services, or related graphics contained in the book for any purpose. Any reliance you place on such information is therefore strictly at your own risk.

JANUARY 1ST

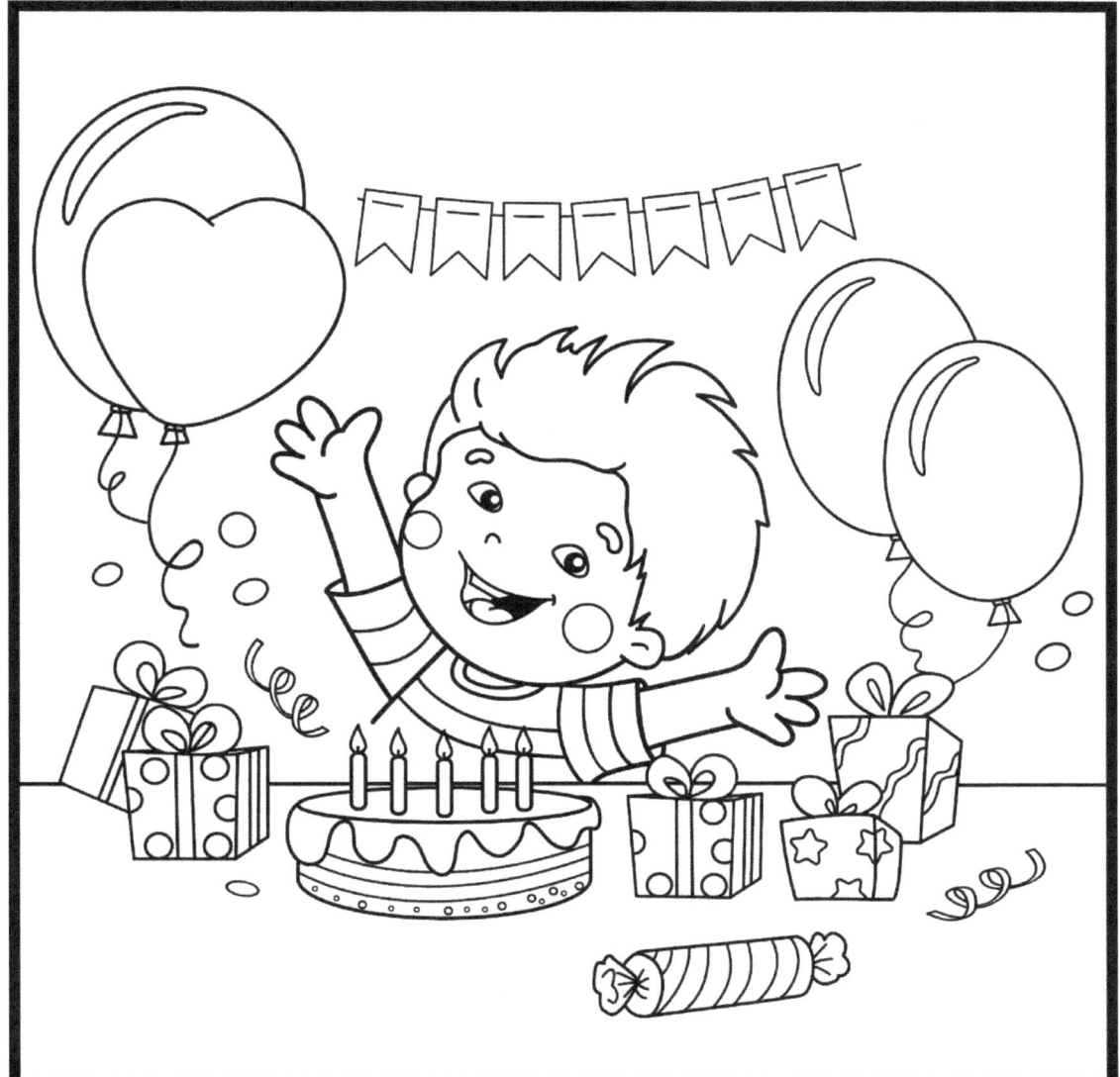

note:

_____

_____

_____

JANUARY 2ND

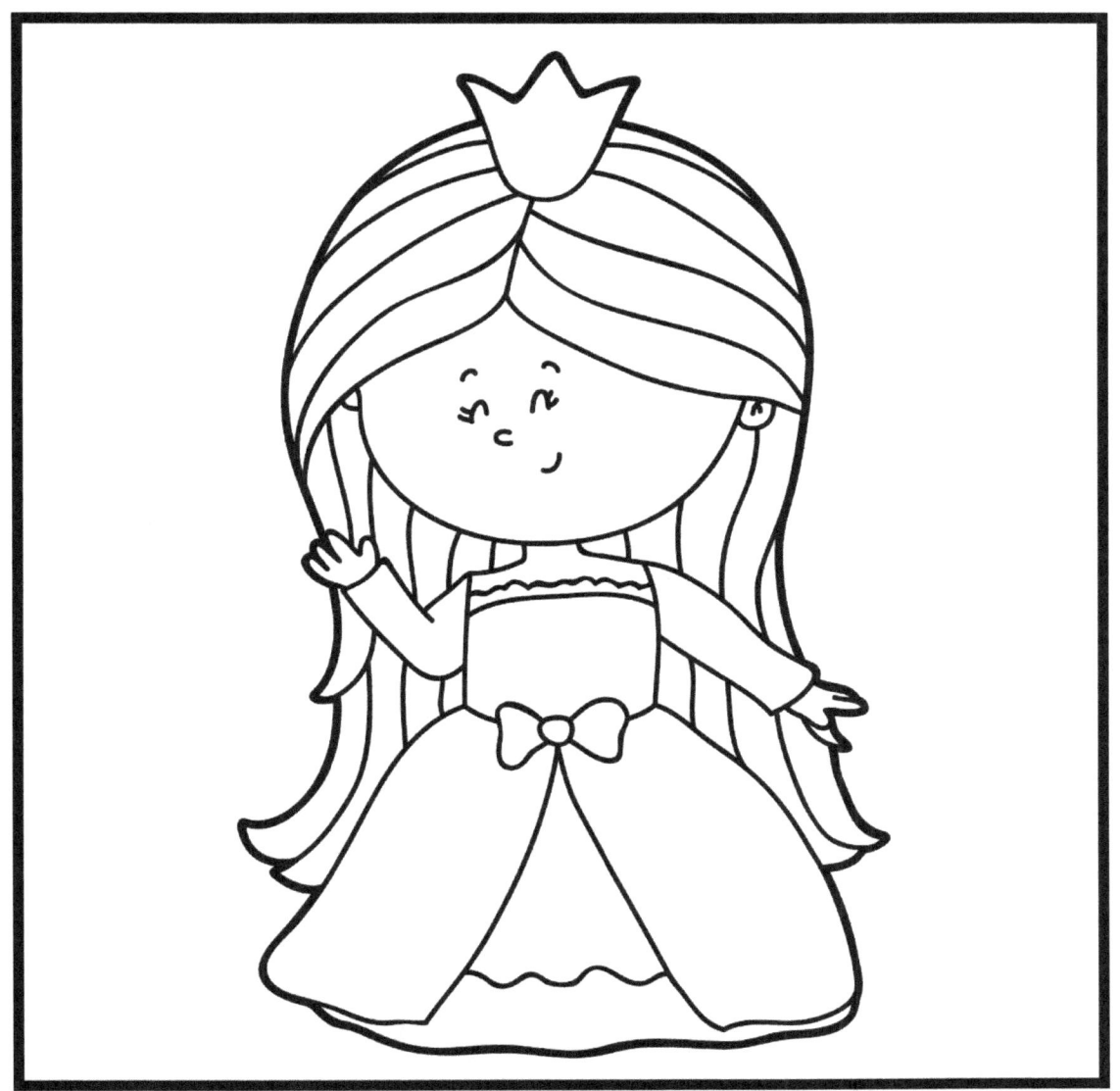

note:

_____

_____

_____

JANUARY 3RD

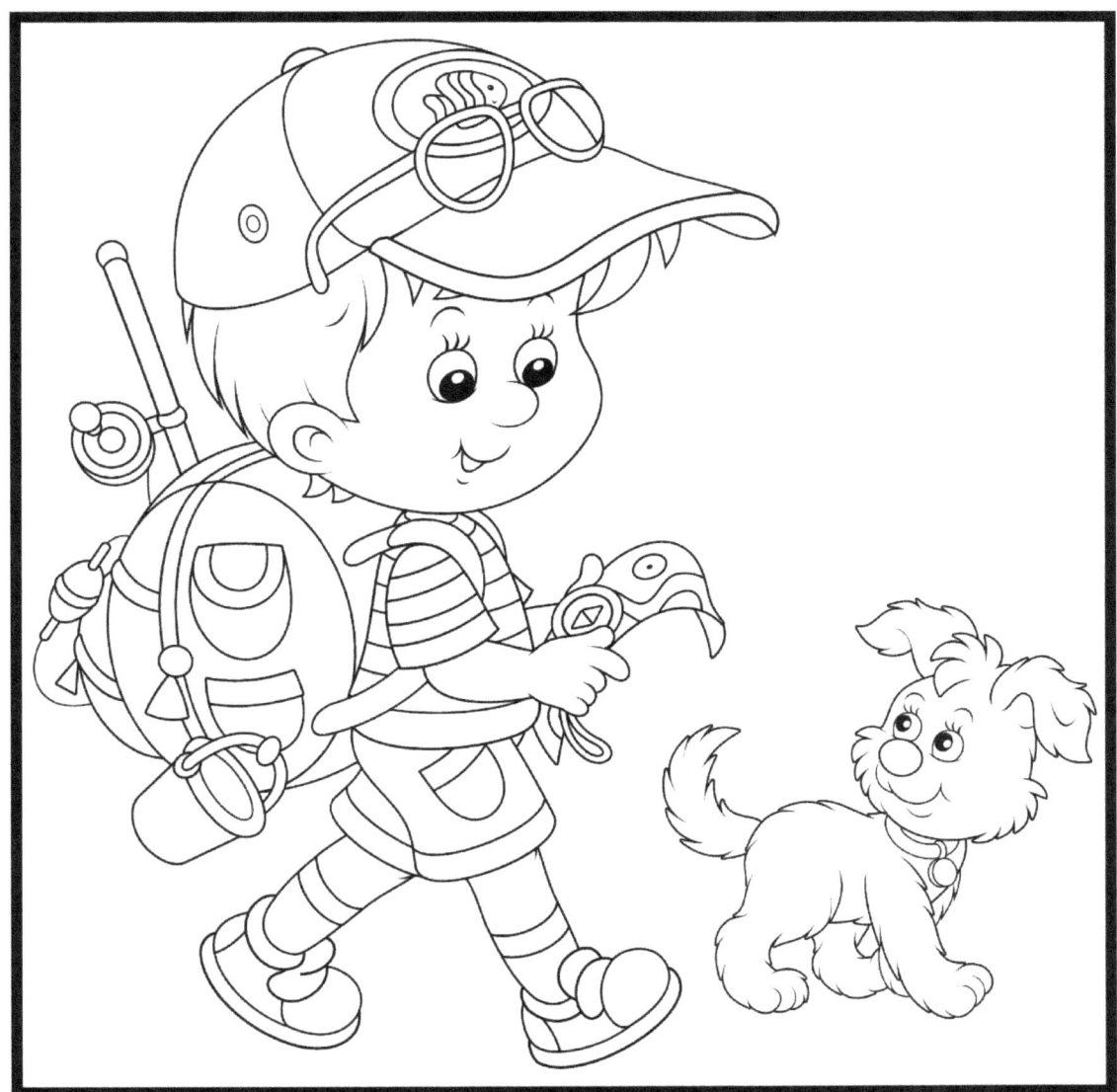

note:

_____

_____

_____

JANUARY 4TH

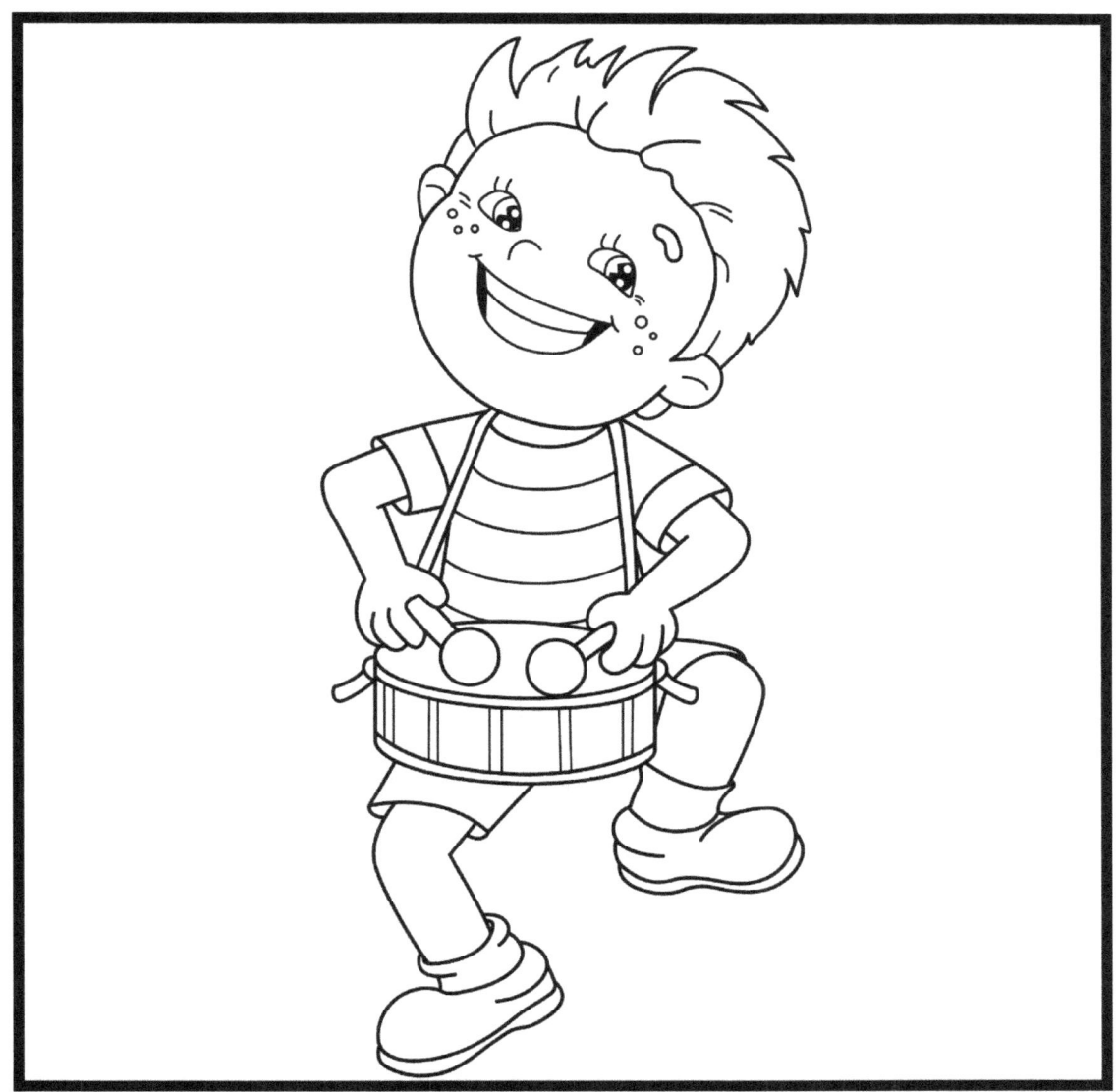

note:

_____

_____

_____

JANUARY 5TH

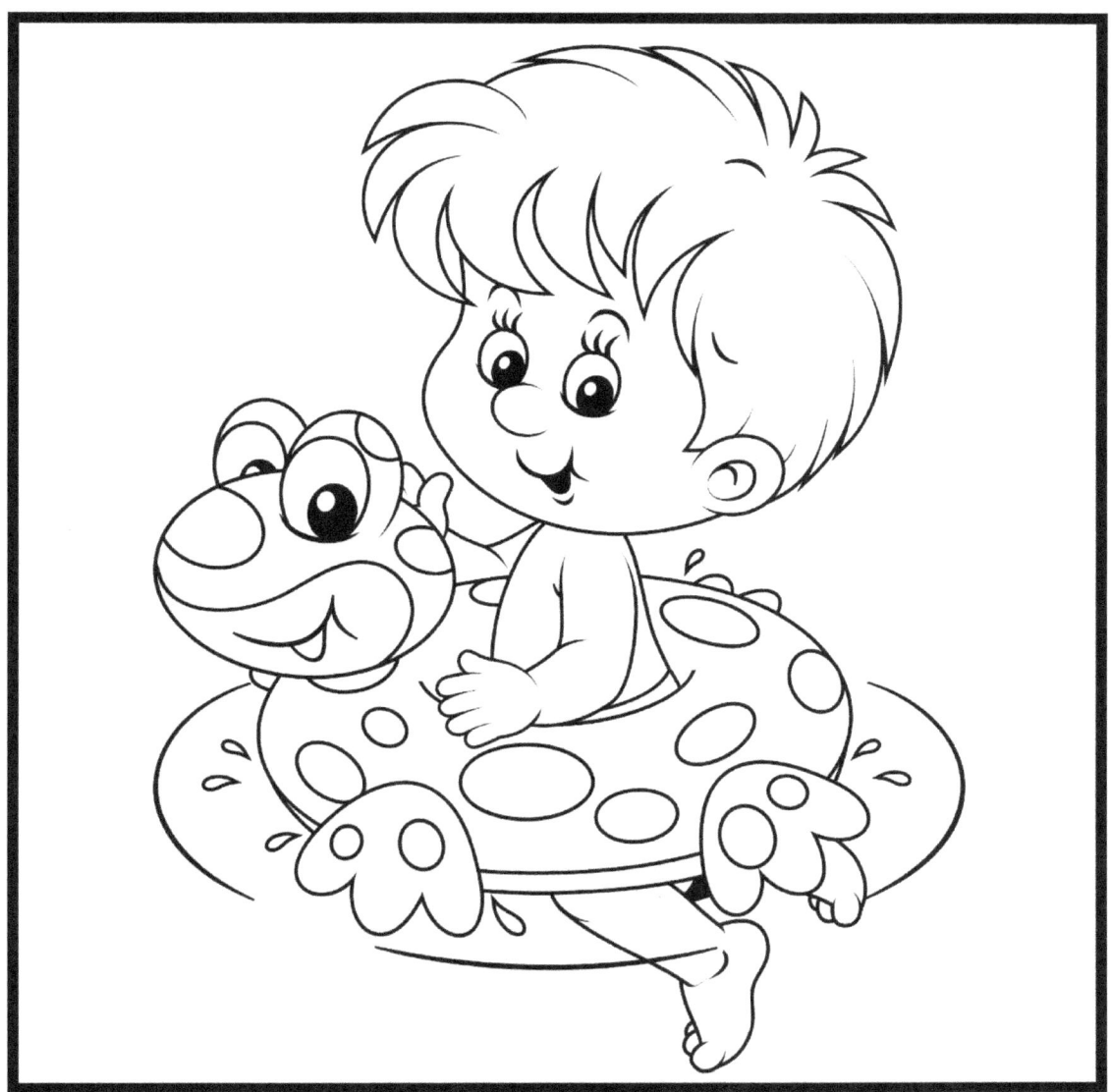

note:

_____

_____

_____

JANUARY 6TH

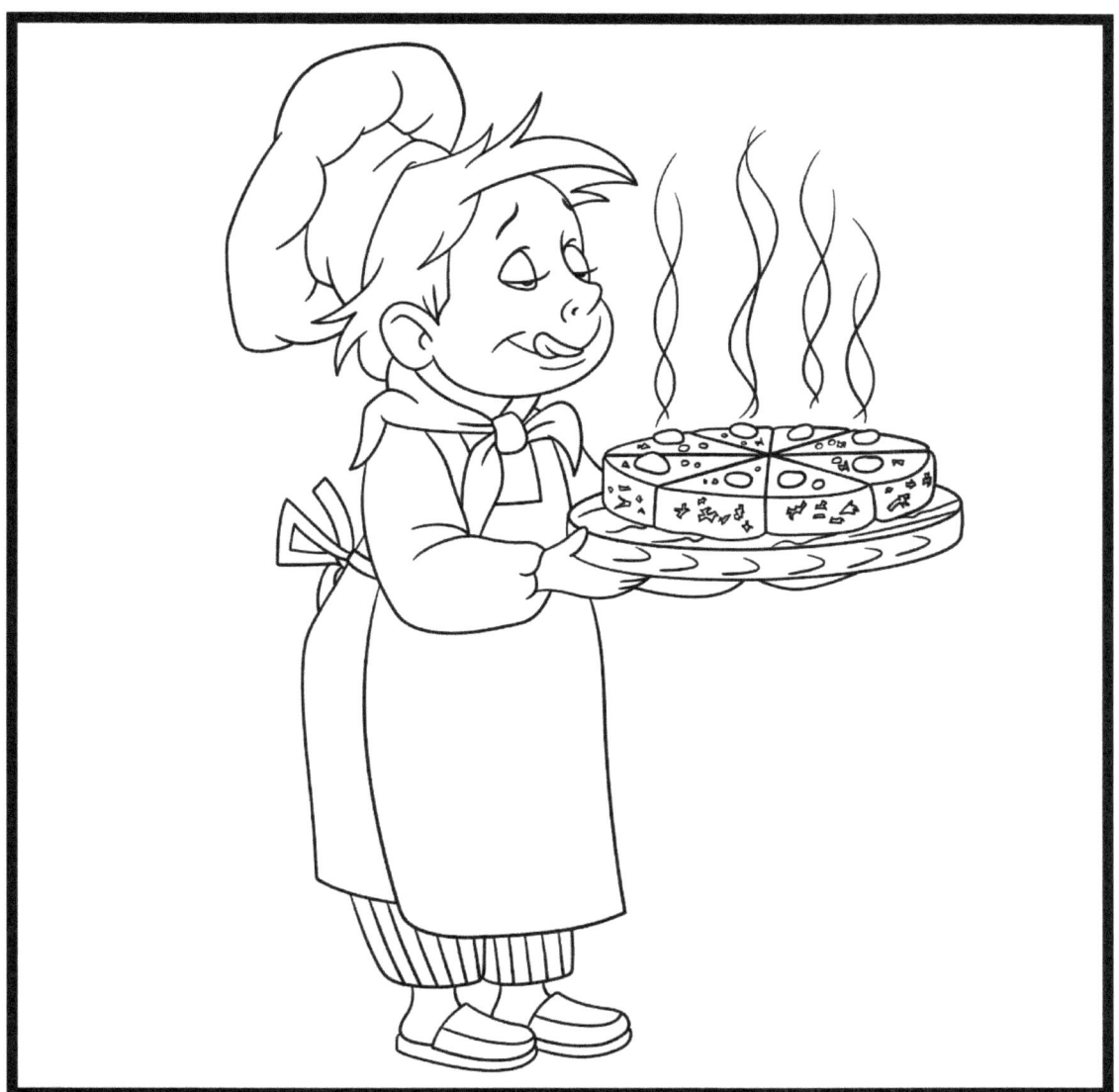

note:

_____

_____

_____

JANUARY 7TH

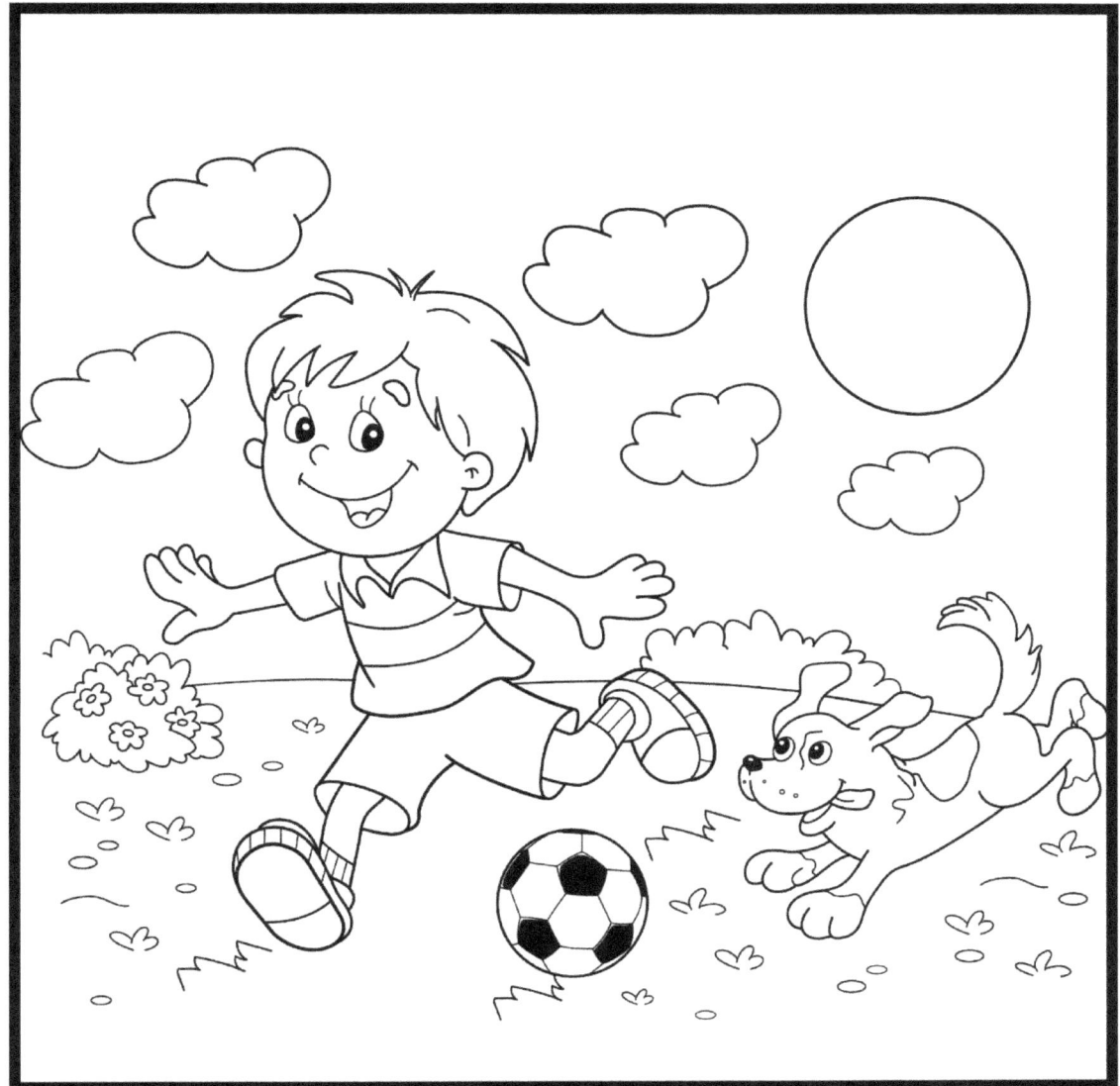

note:

_____

_____

_____

JANUARY 8TH

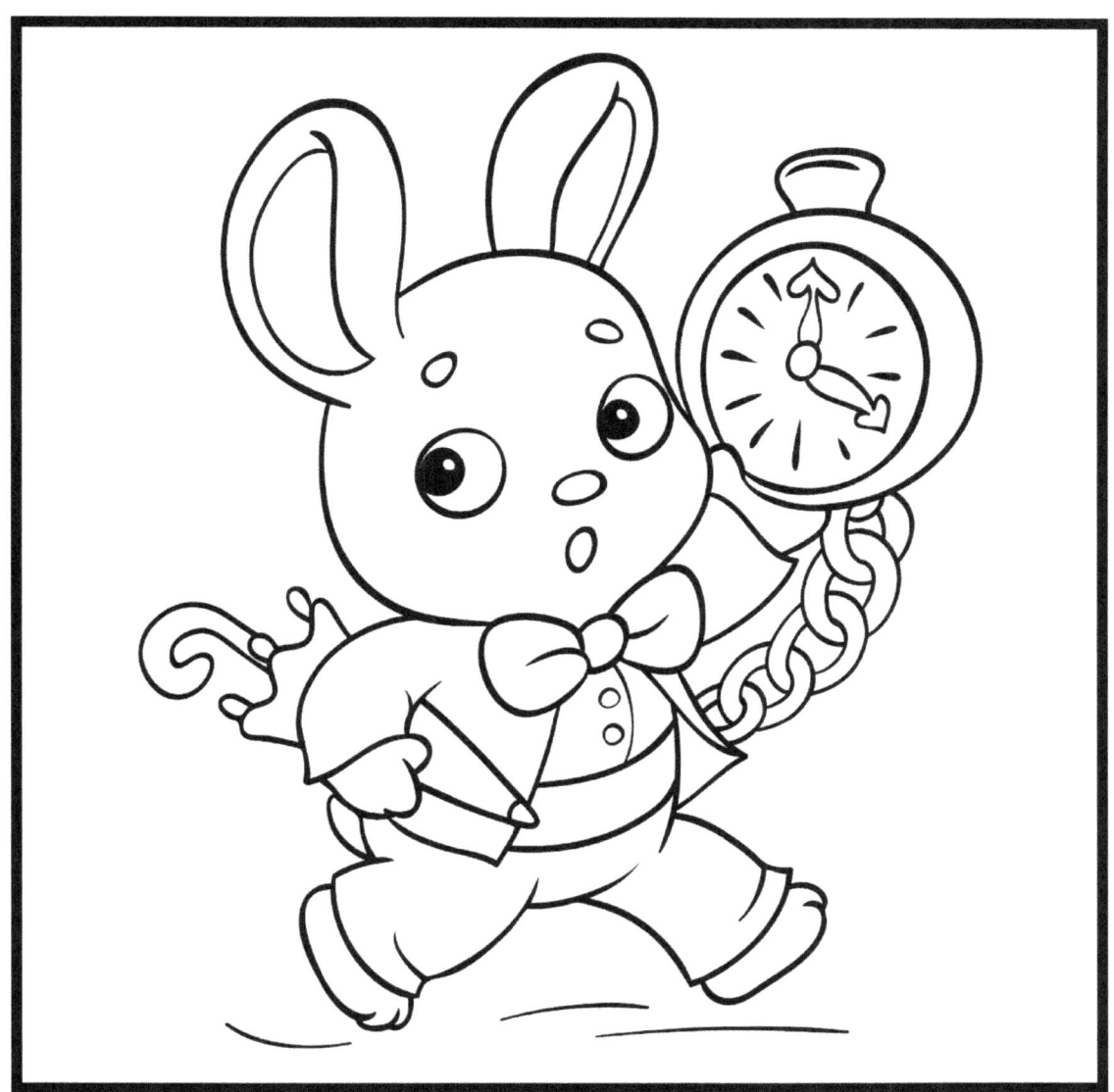

note:

_____

_____

_____

JANUARY 9TH

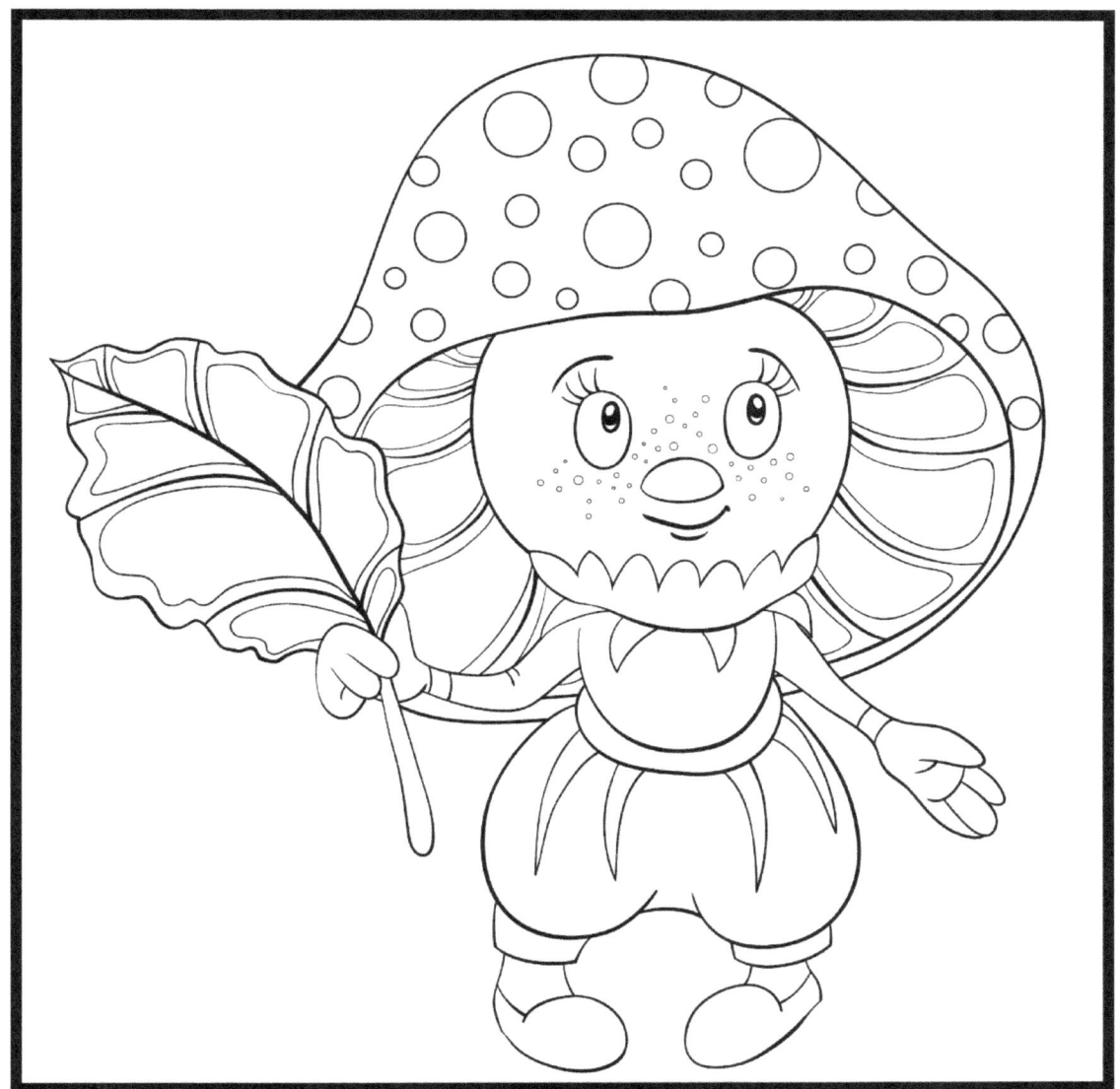

note:

_____

_____

_____

JANUARY 10TH

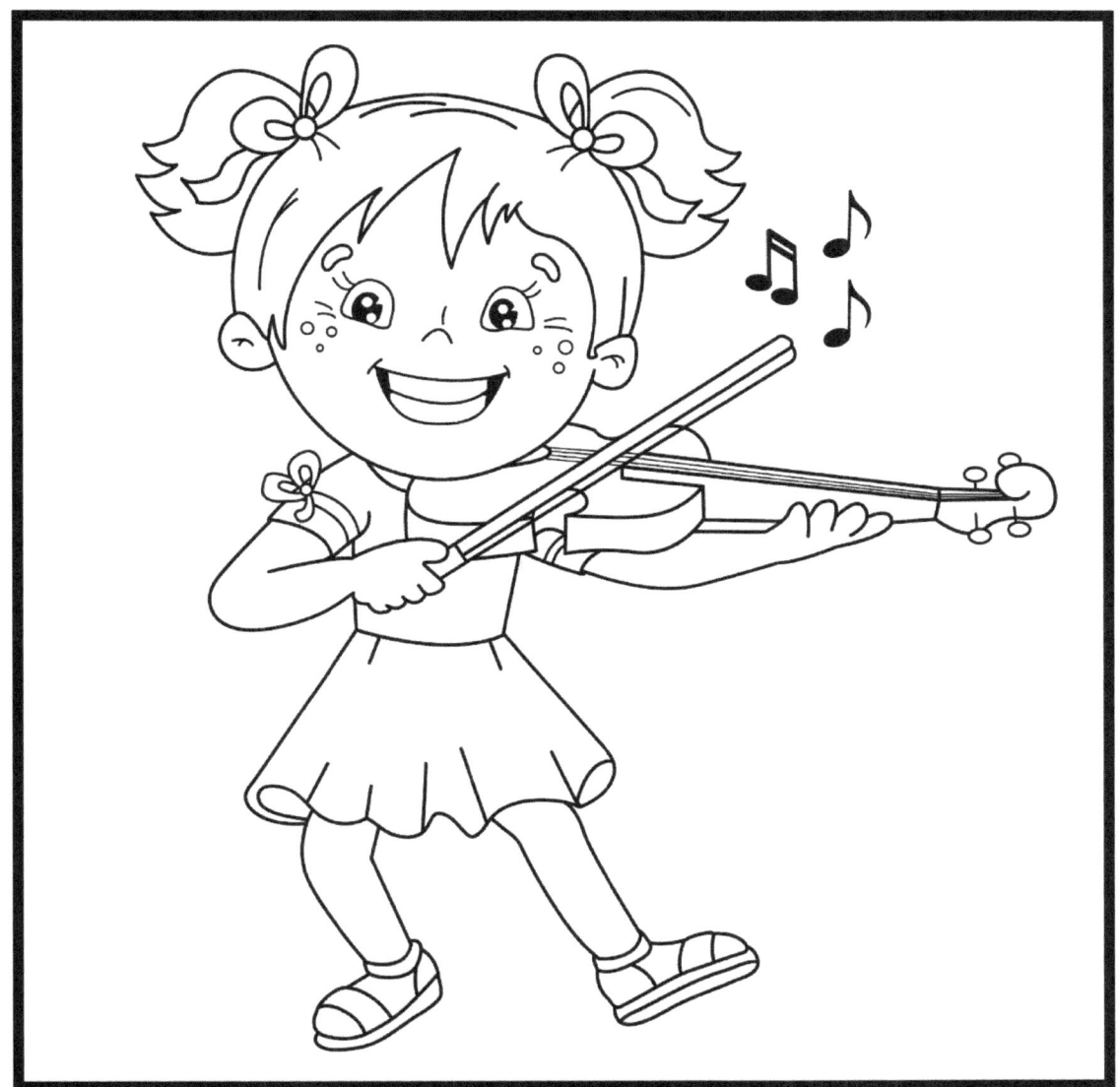

note:

_____

_____

_____

JANUARY 11TH

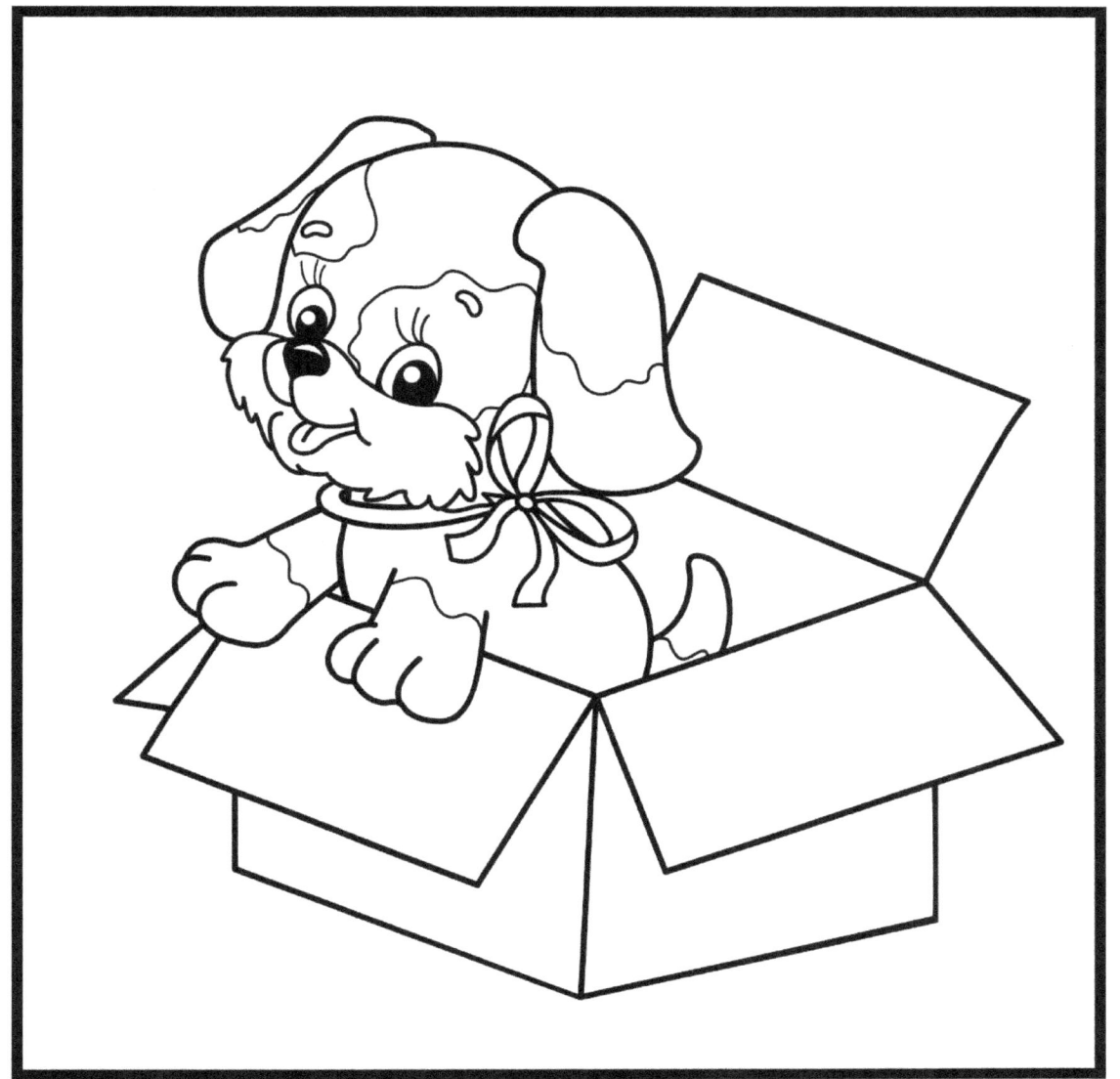

note:

_____

_____

_____

JANUARY 12TH

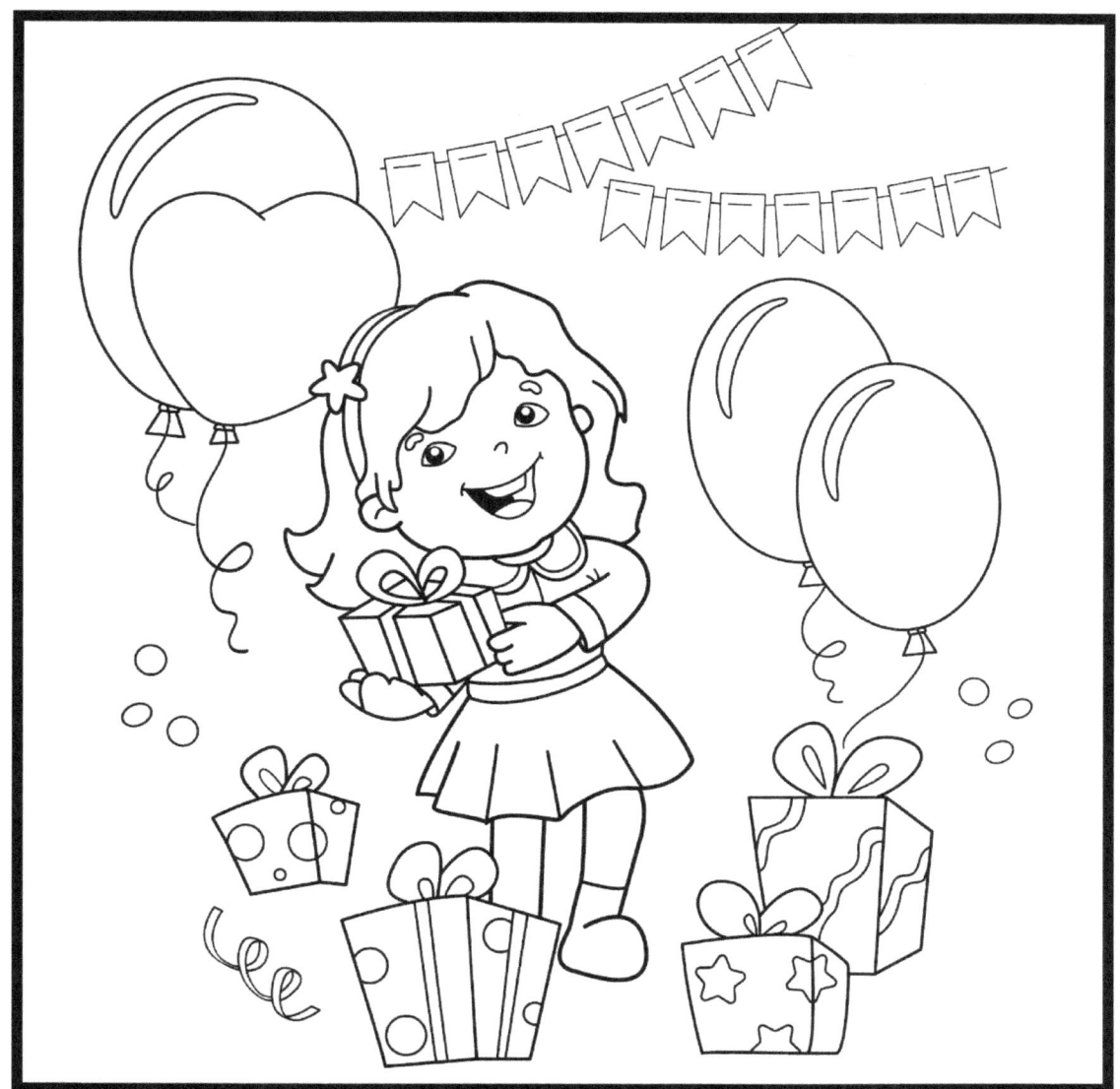

note:

_____

_____

_____

JANUARY 13TH

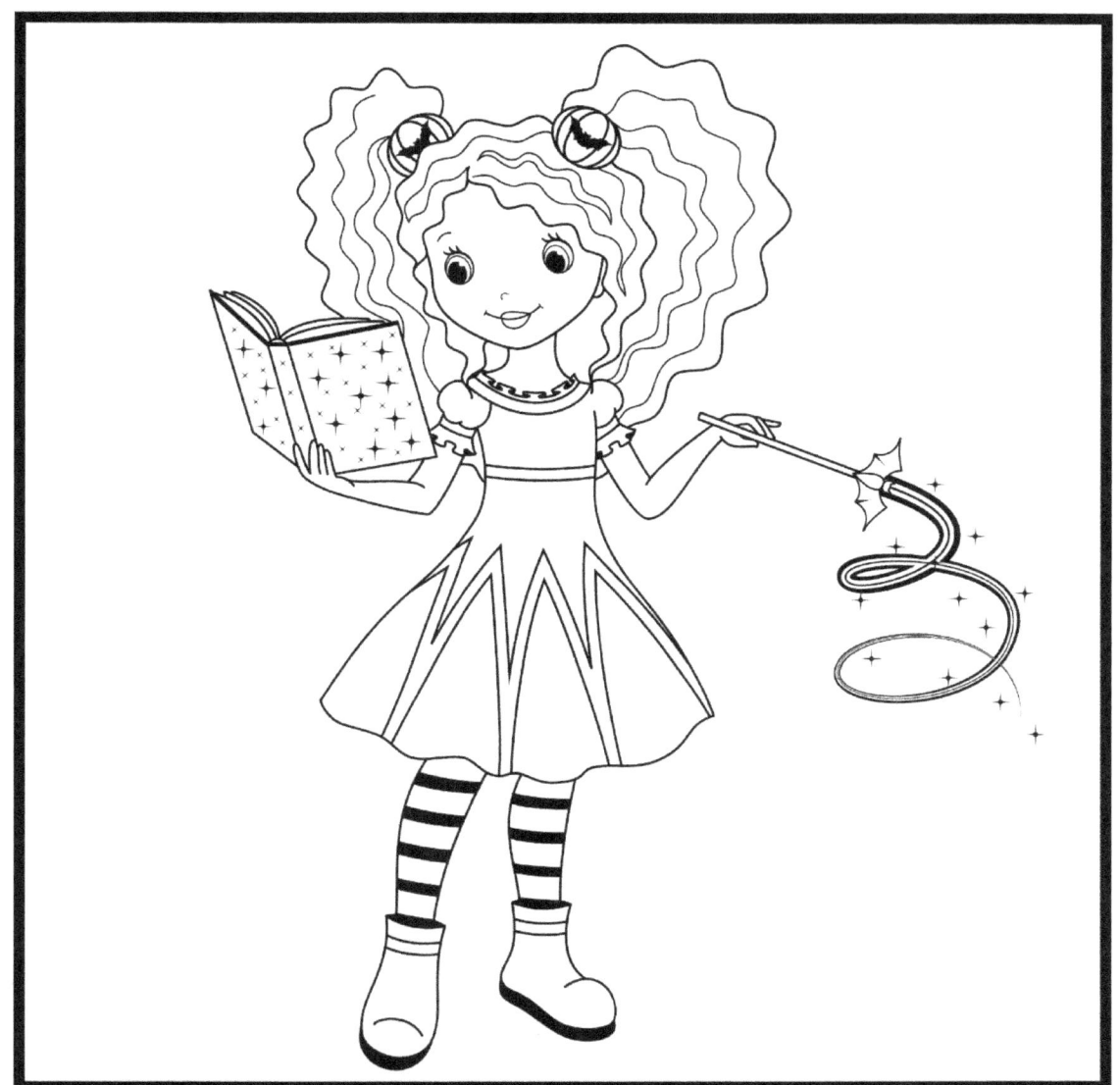

note:

_____

_____

_____

JANUARY 14TH

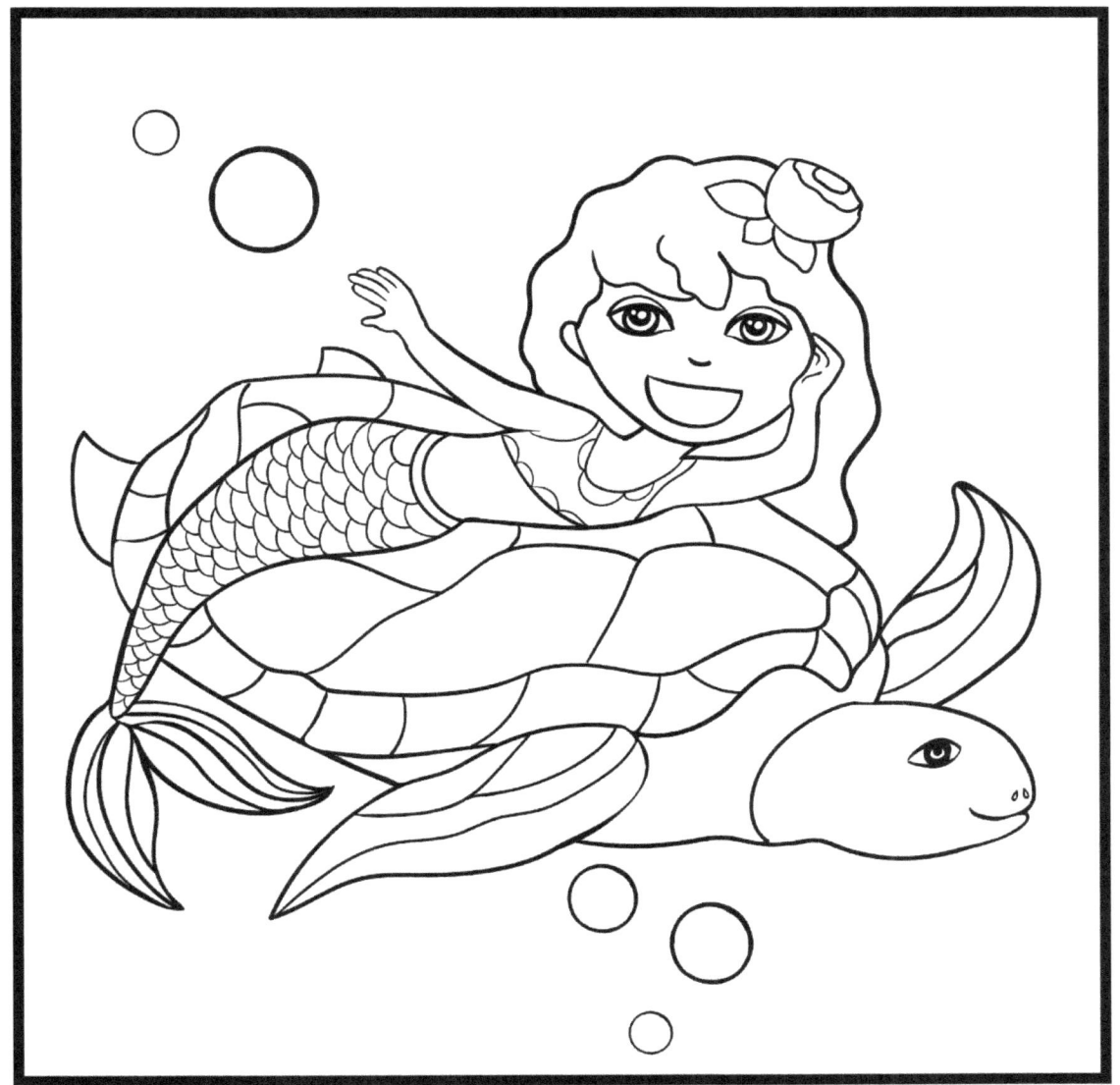

note:

_____

_____

_____

JANUARY 15TH

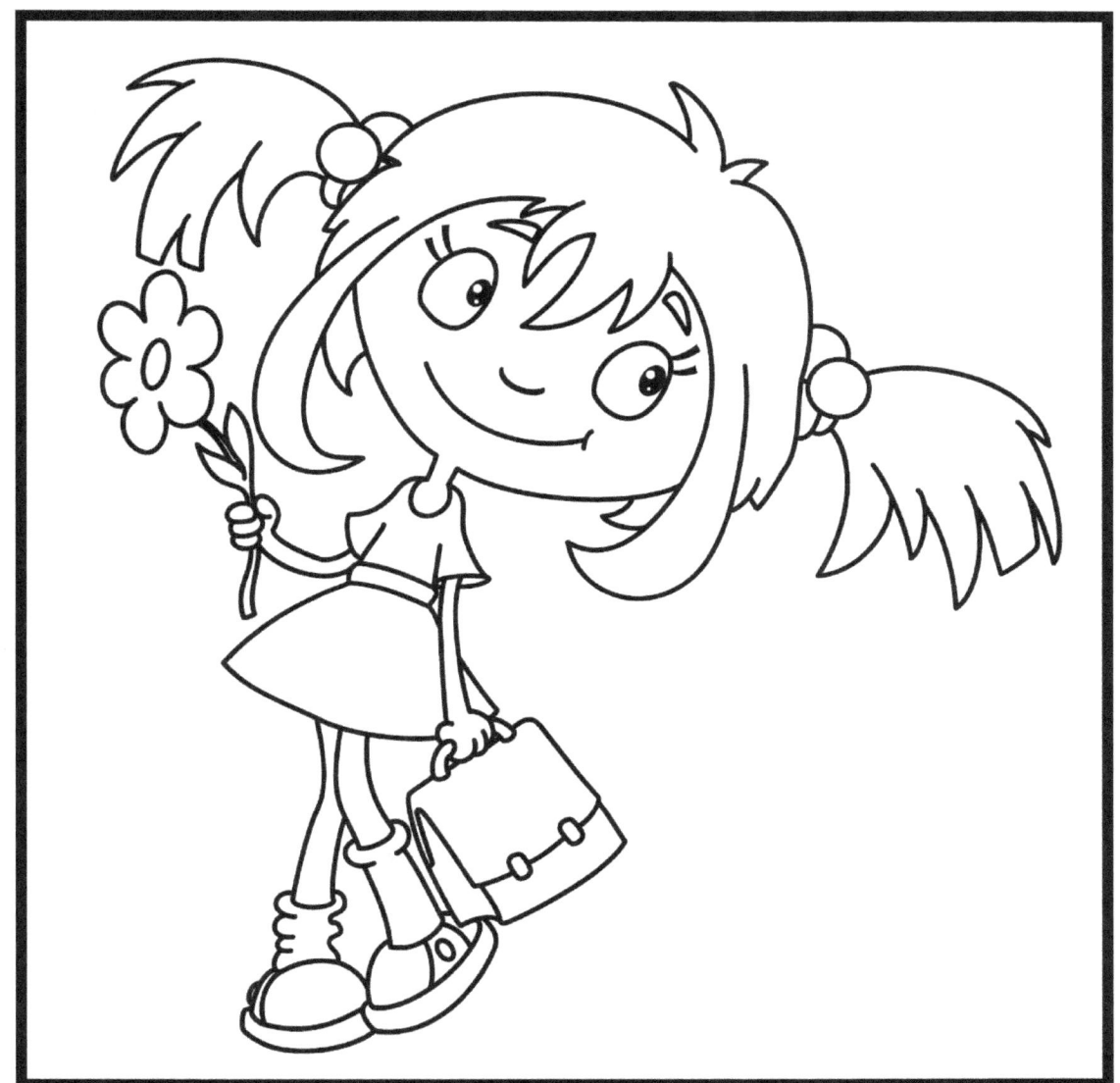

note:

_____

_____

_____

JANUARY 16TH

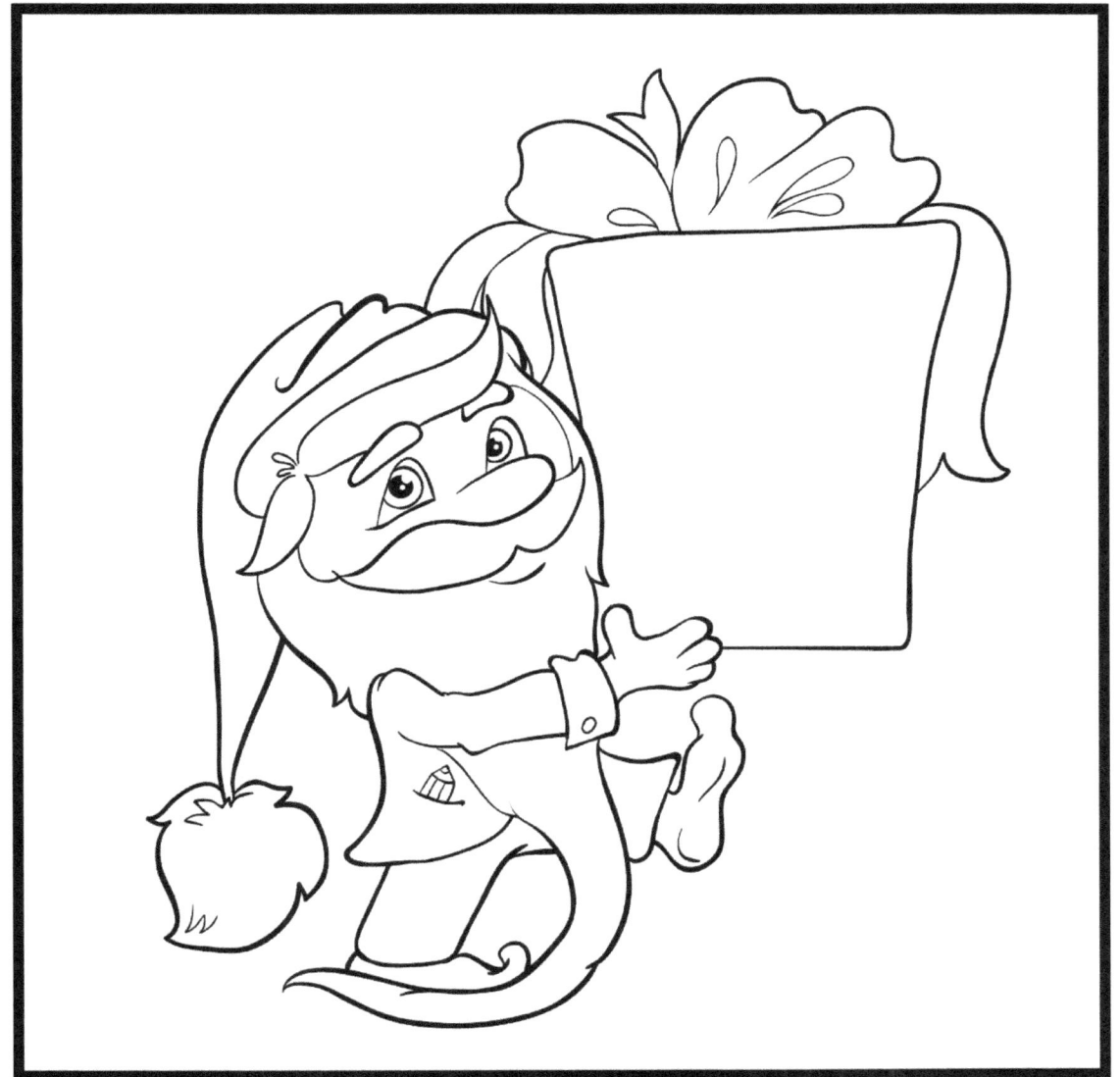

note:

_____

_____

_____

JANUARY 17TH

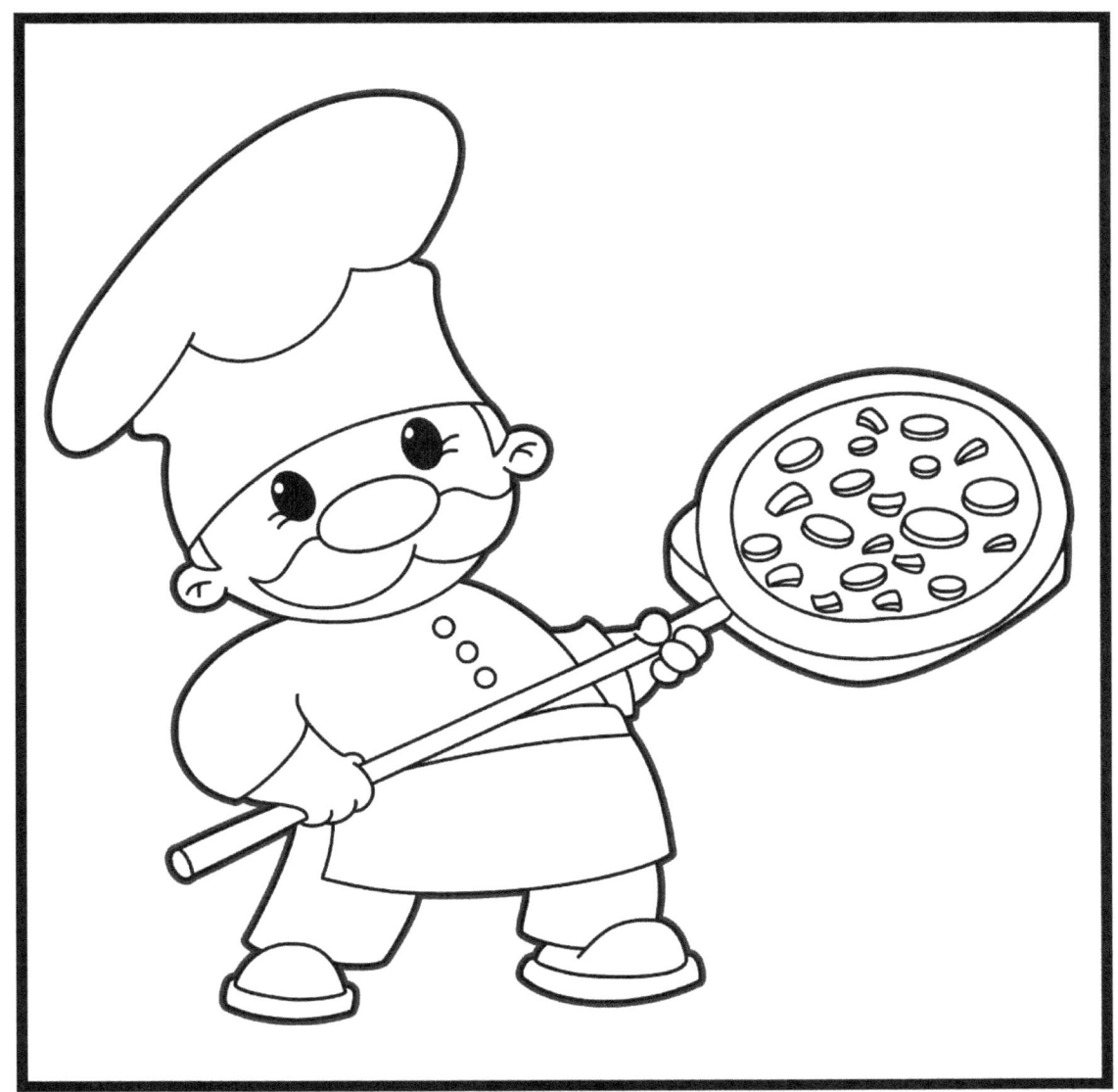

note:

_____

_____

_____

JANUARY 18TH

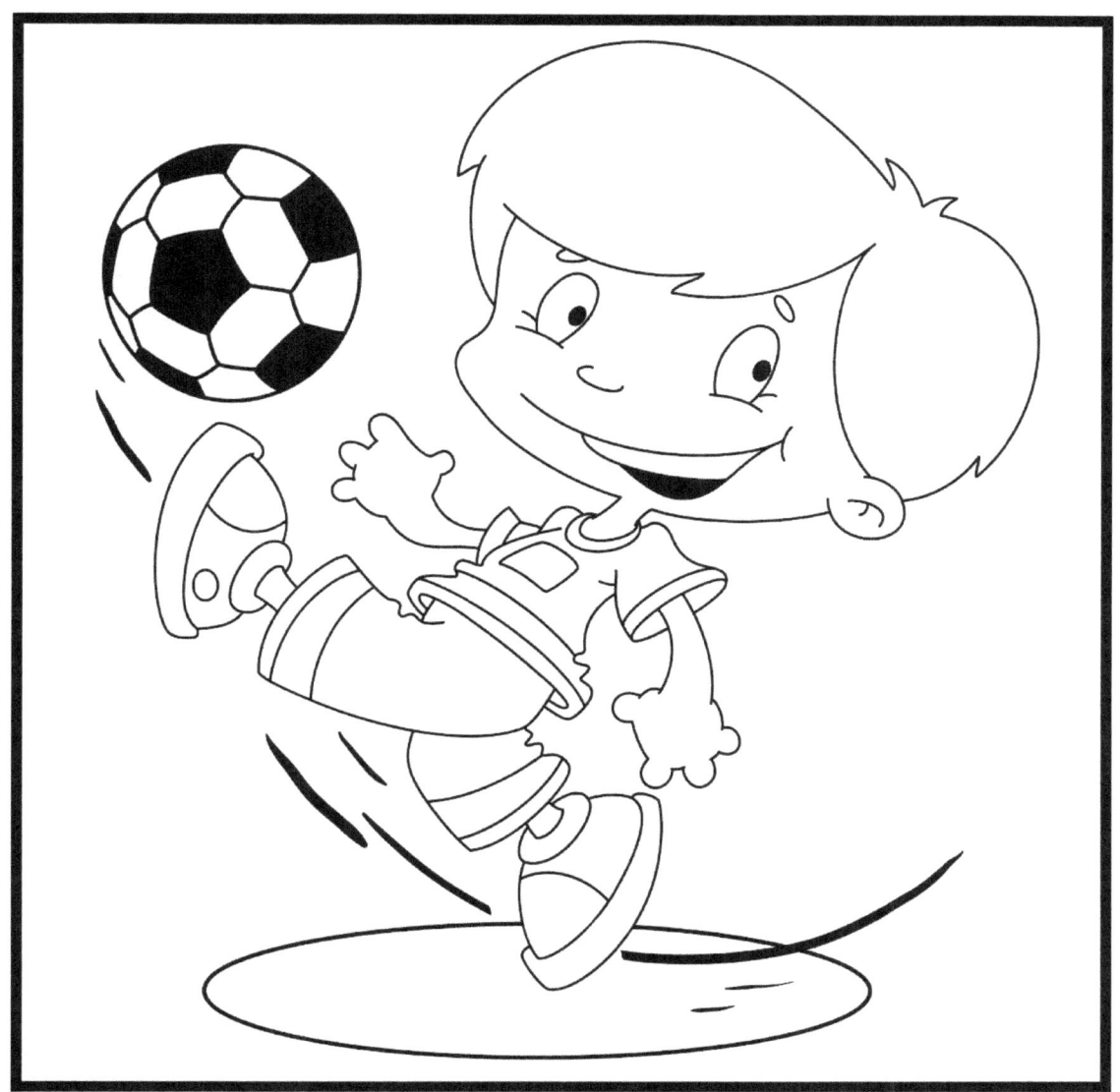

note:

_____

_____

_____

JANUARY 19TH

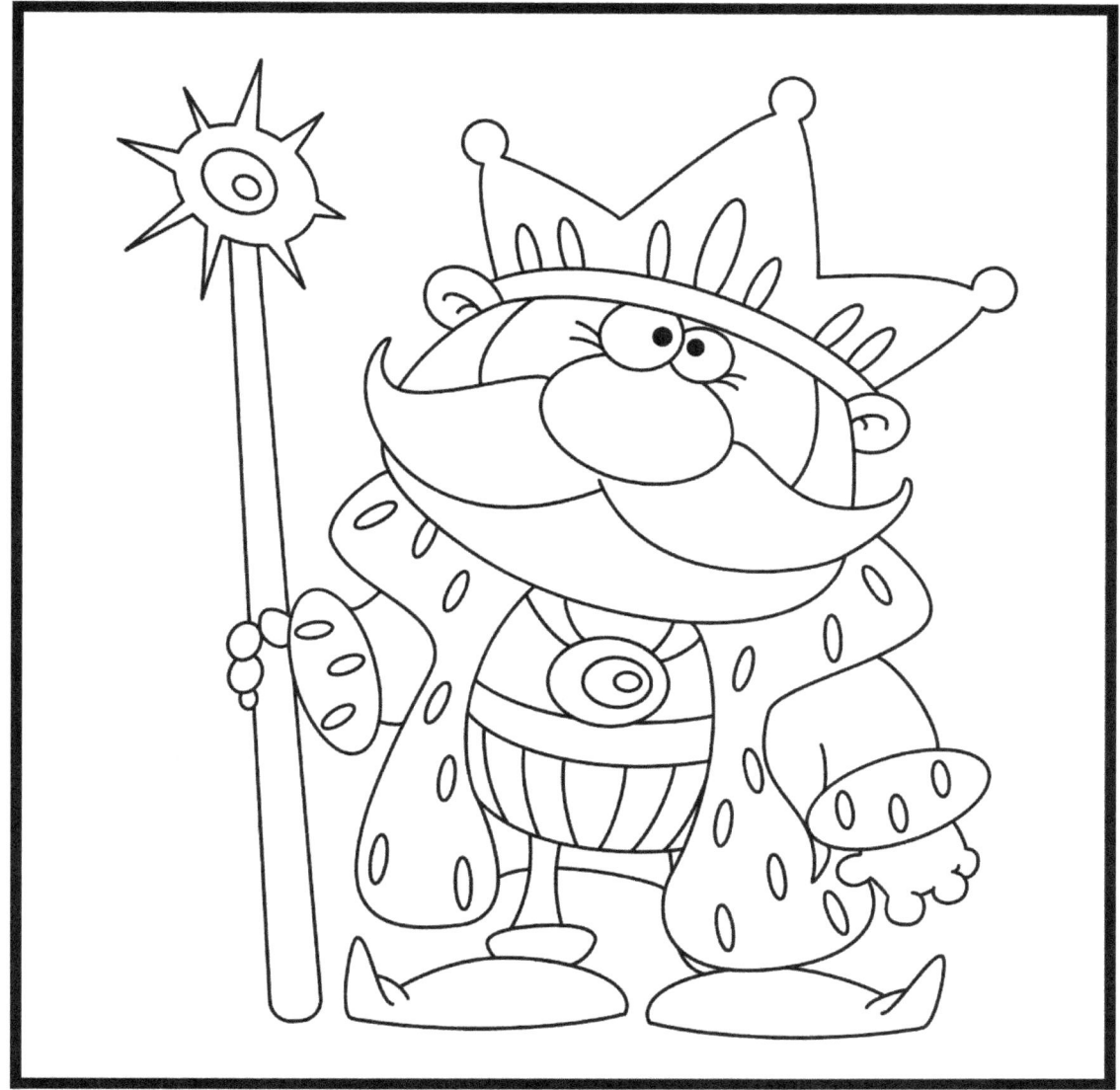

note:

_____

_____

_____

JANUARY 20TH

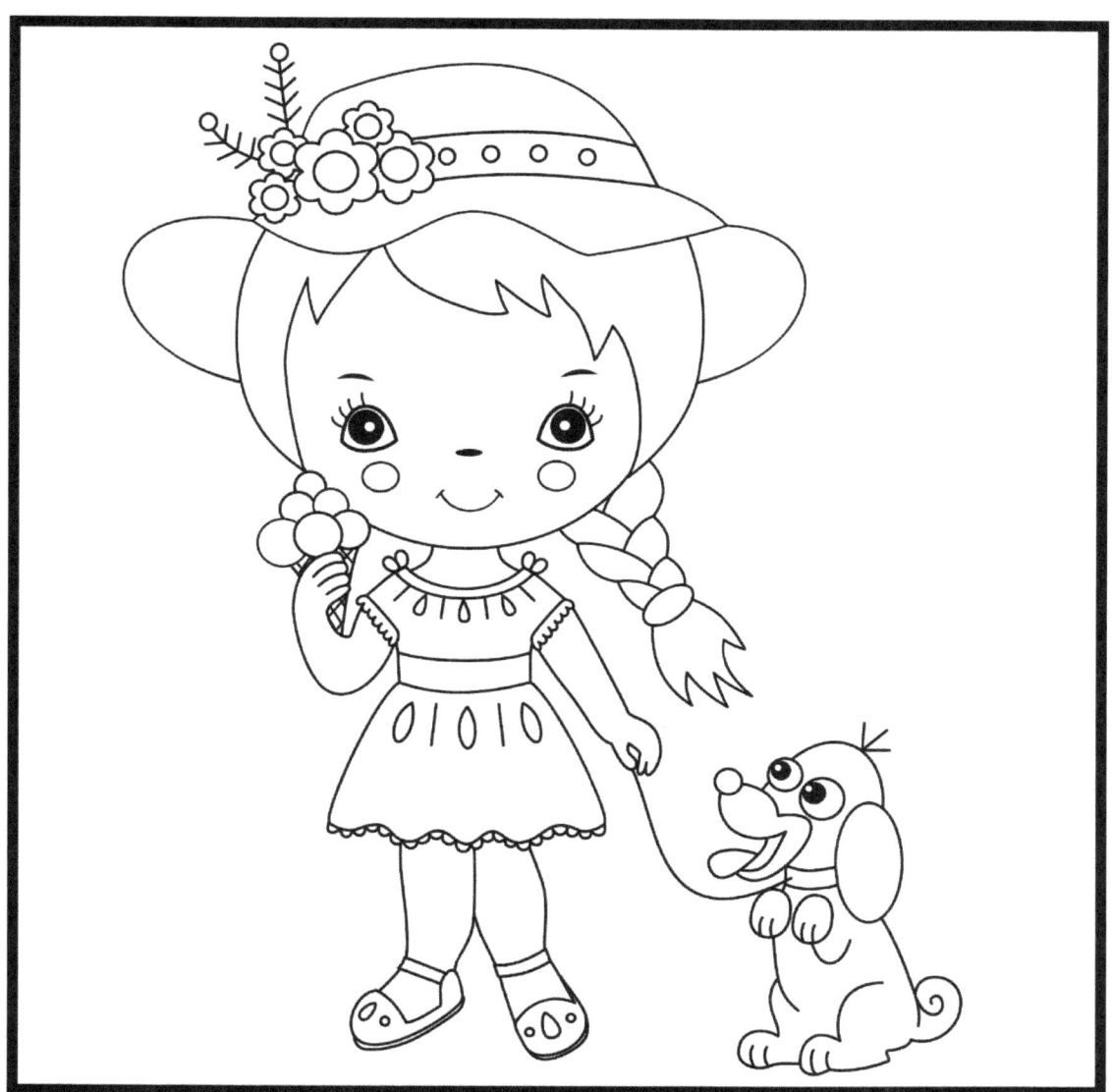

note:

_____

_____

_____

JANUARY 21TH

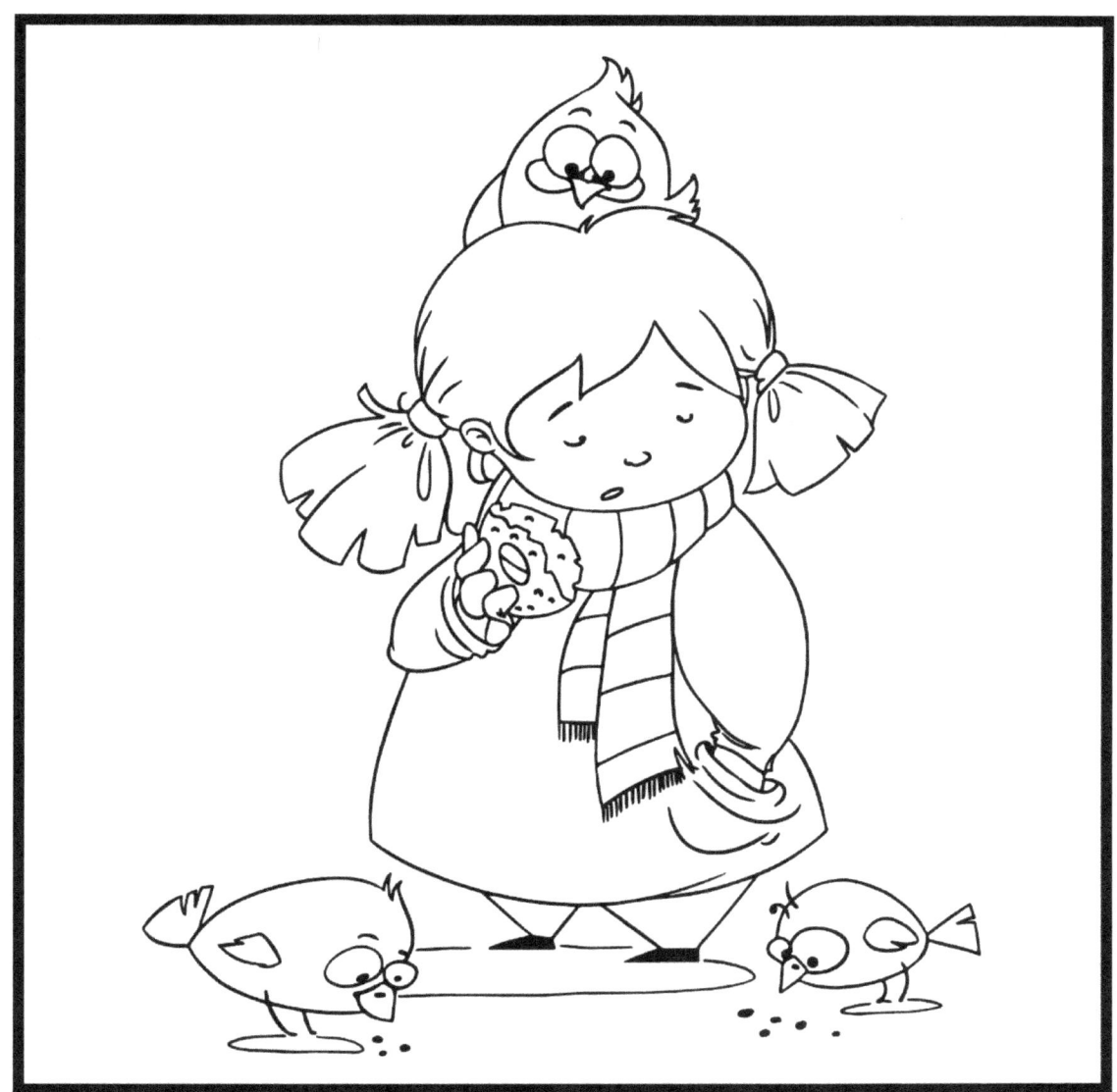

note:

_____

_____

_____

JANUARY 22TH

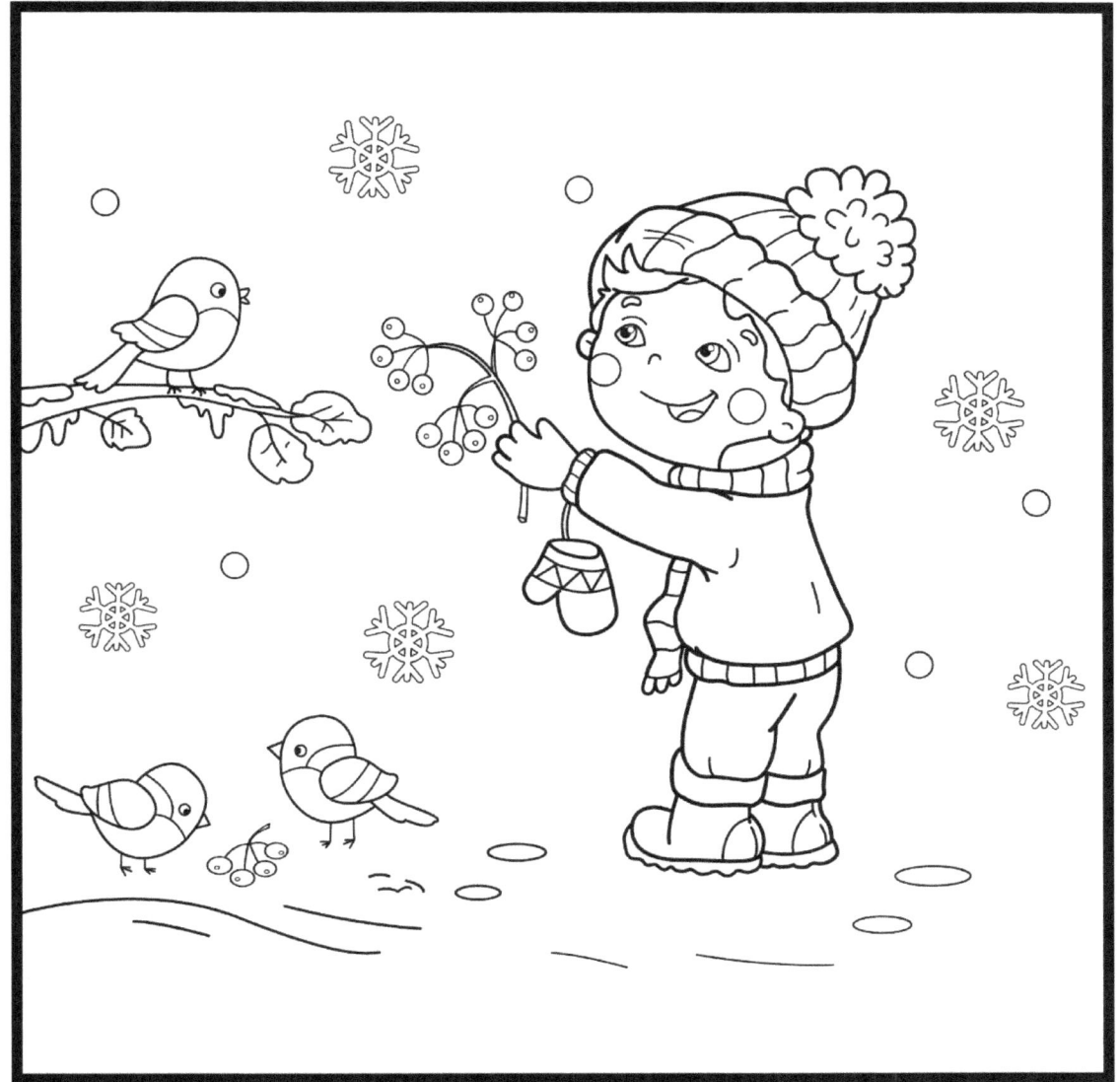

note:

_____

_____

_____

JANUARY 23TH

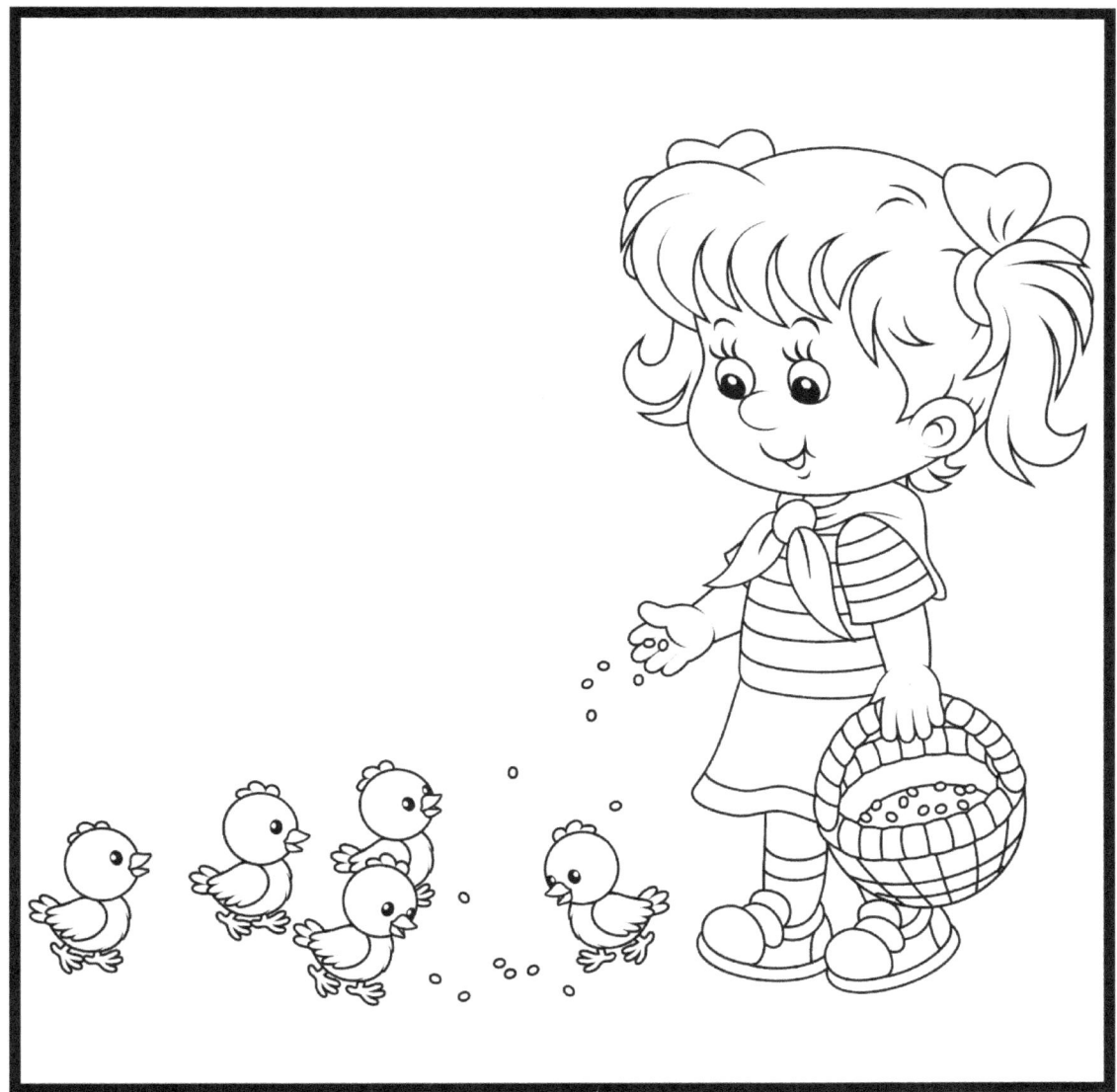

note:

_____

_____

_____

JANUARY 24TH

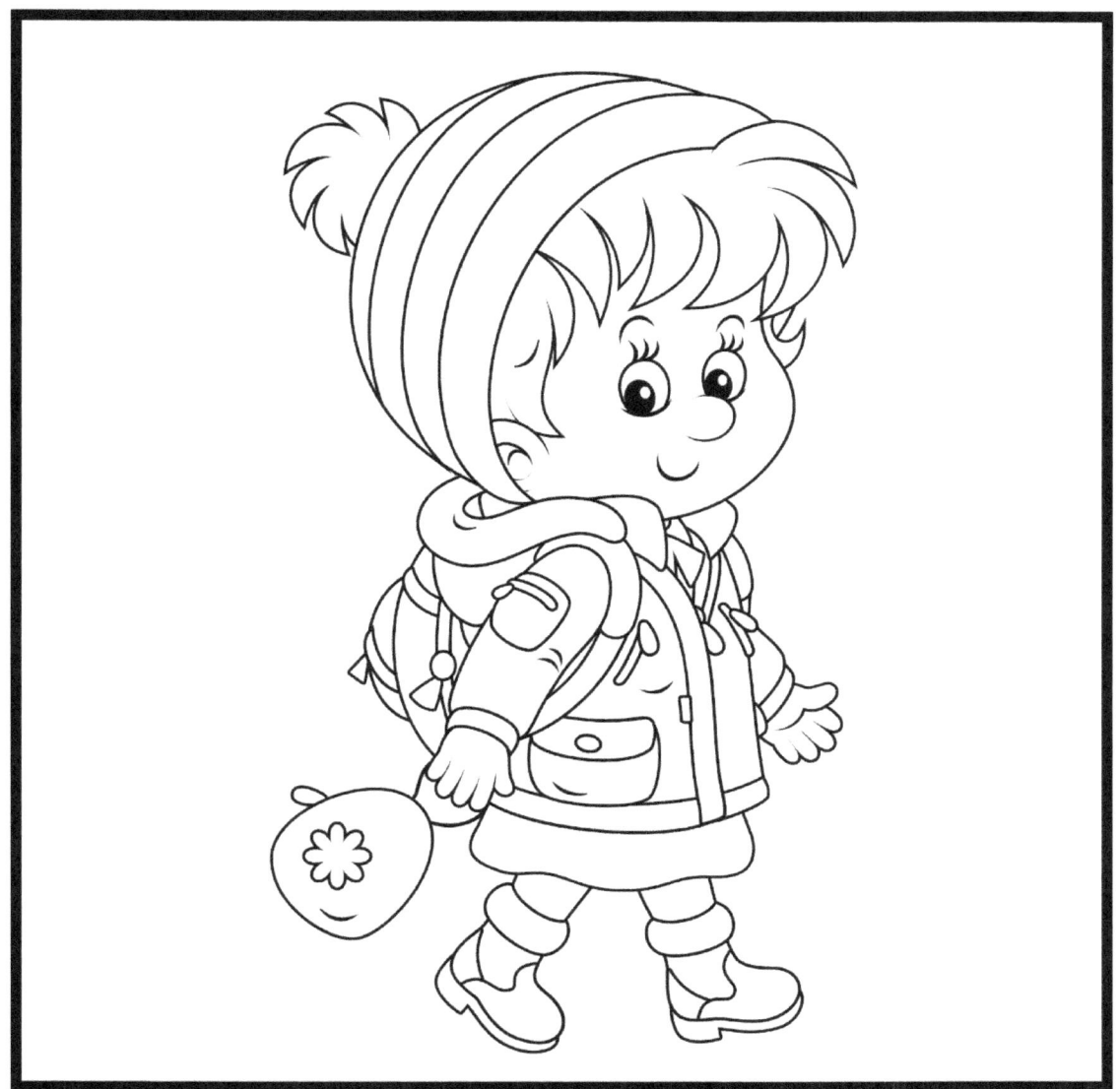

note:

_____

_____

_____

JANUARY 25TH

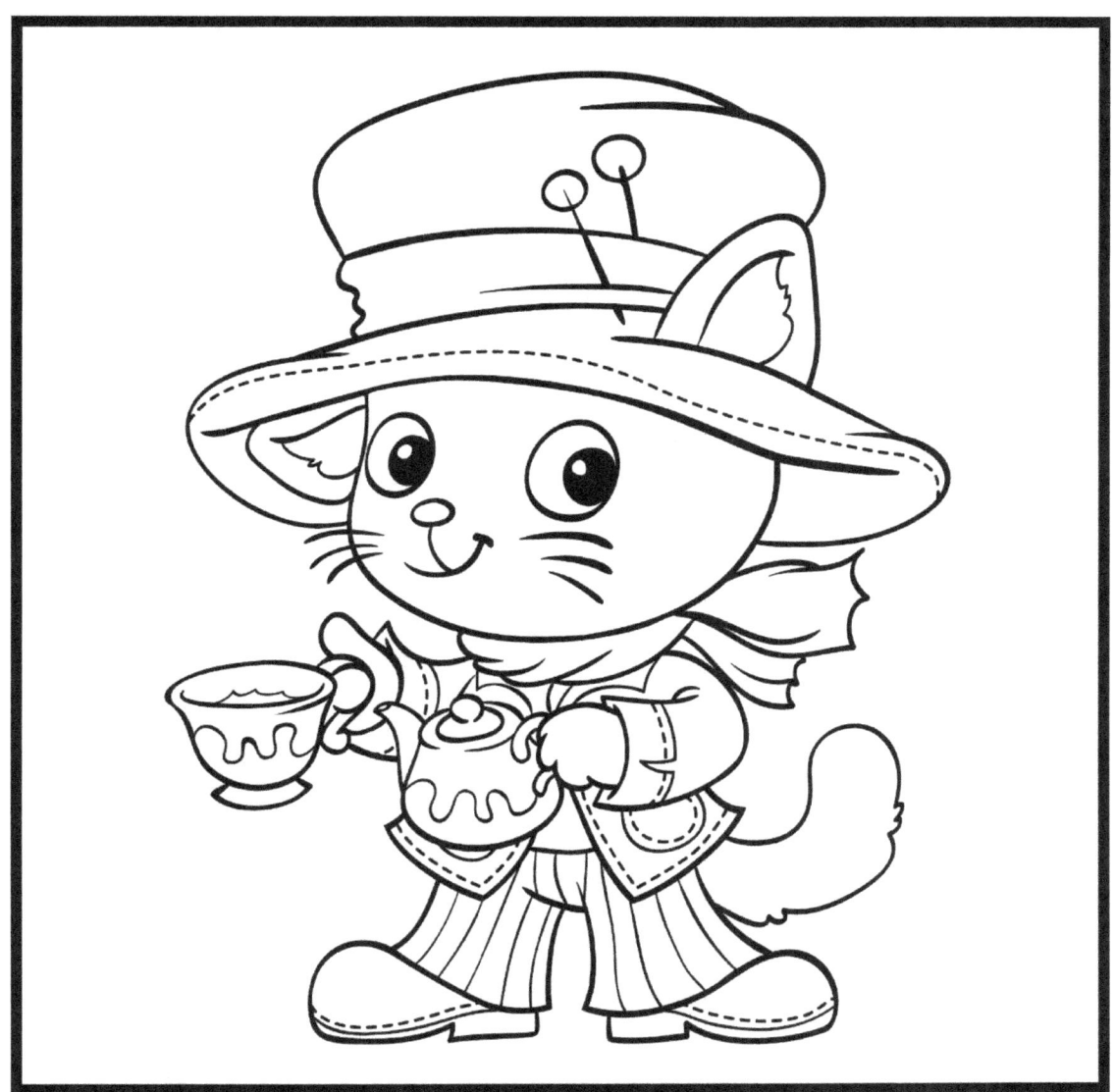

note:

_____

_____

_____

JANUARY 26TH

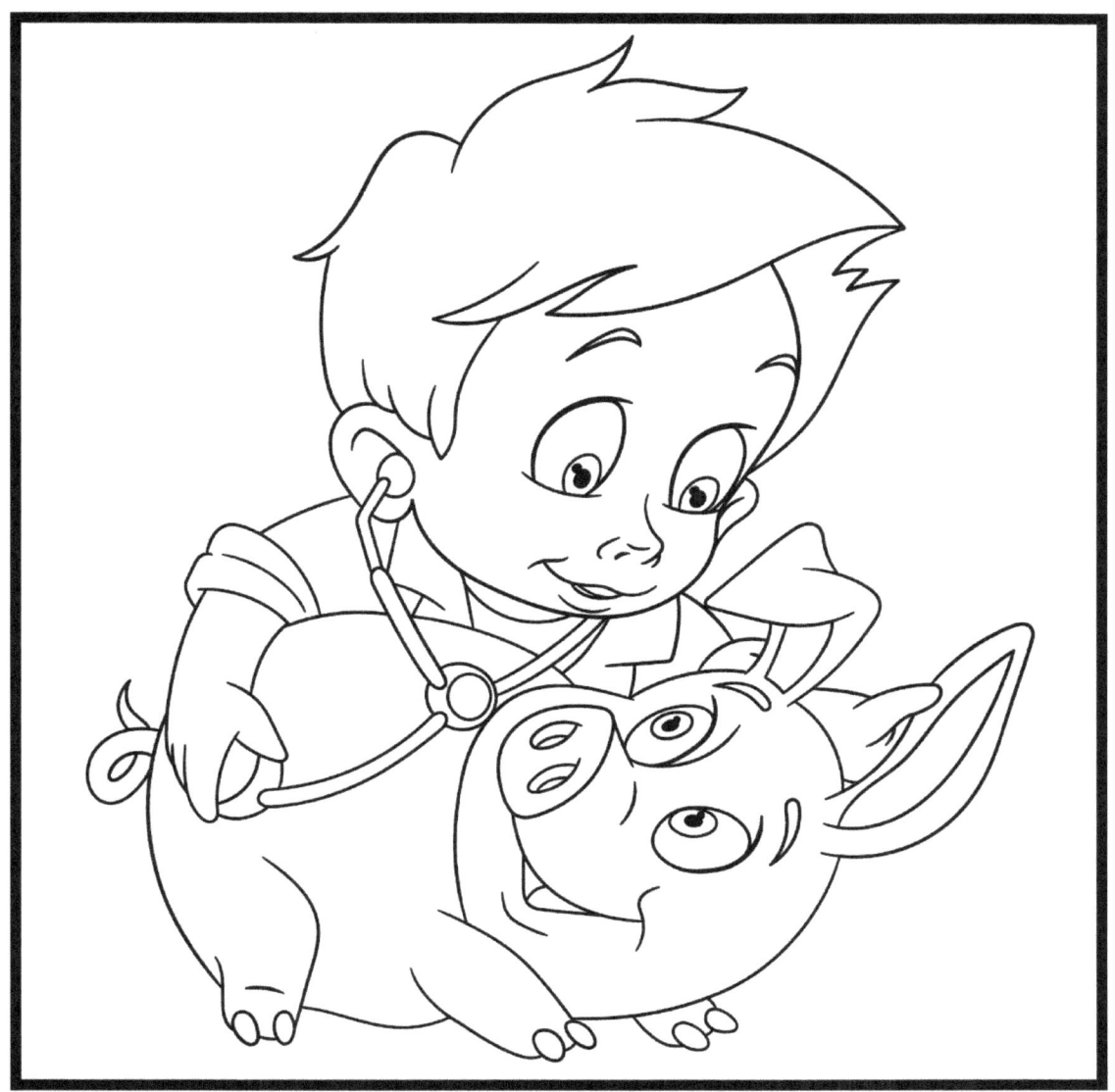

note:

_____

_____

_____

JANUARY 27TH

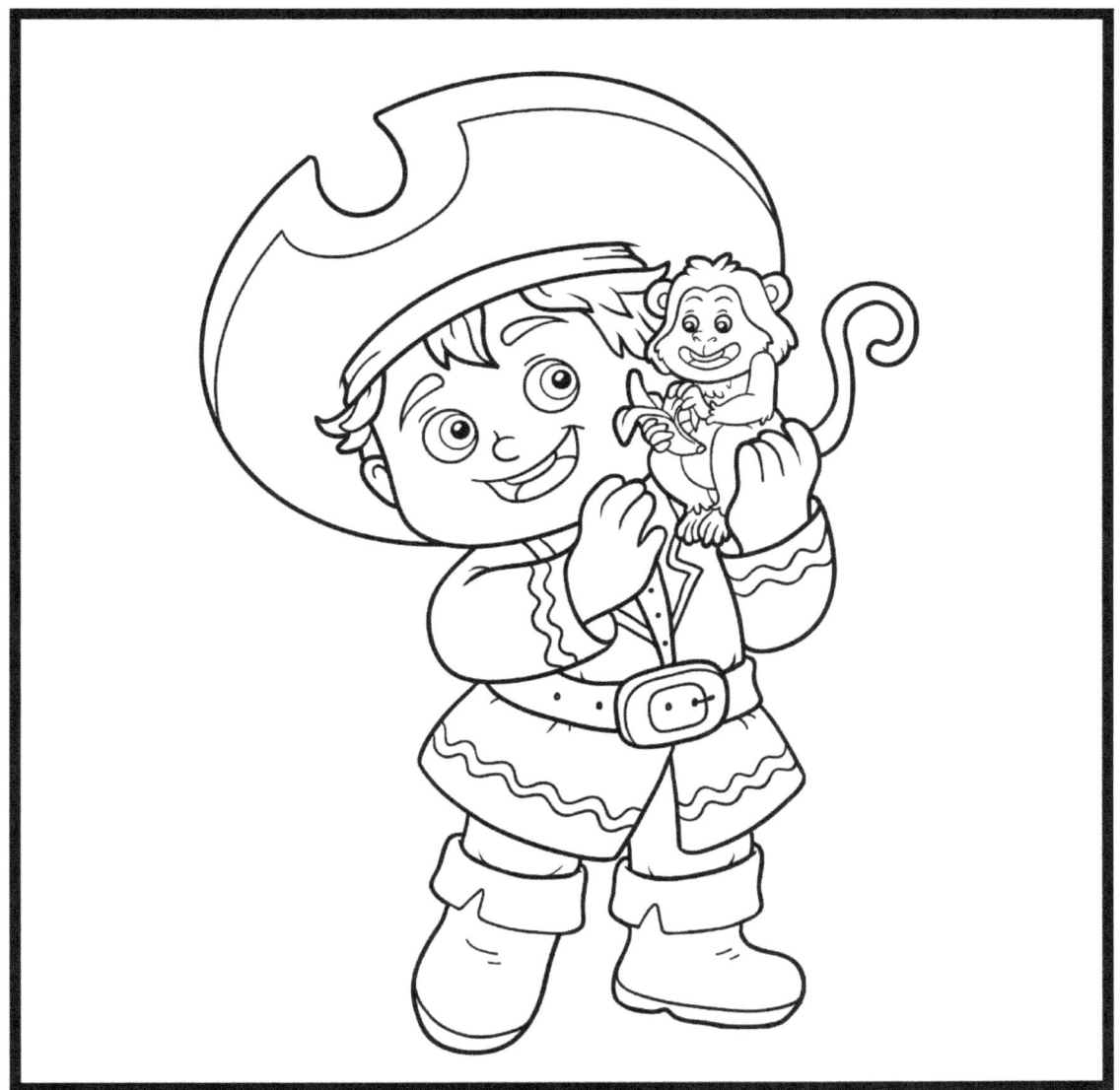

note:

_____

_____

_____

JANUARY 28TH

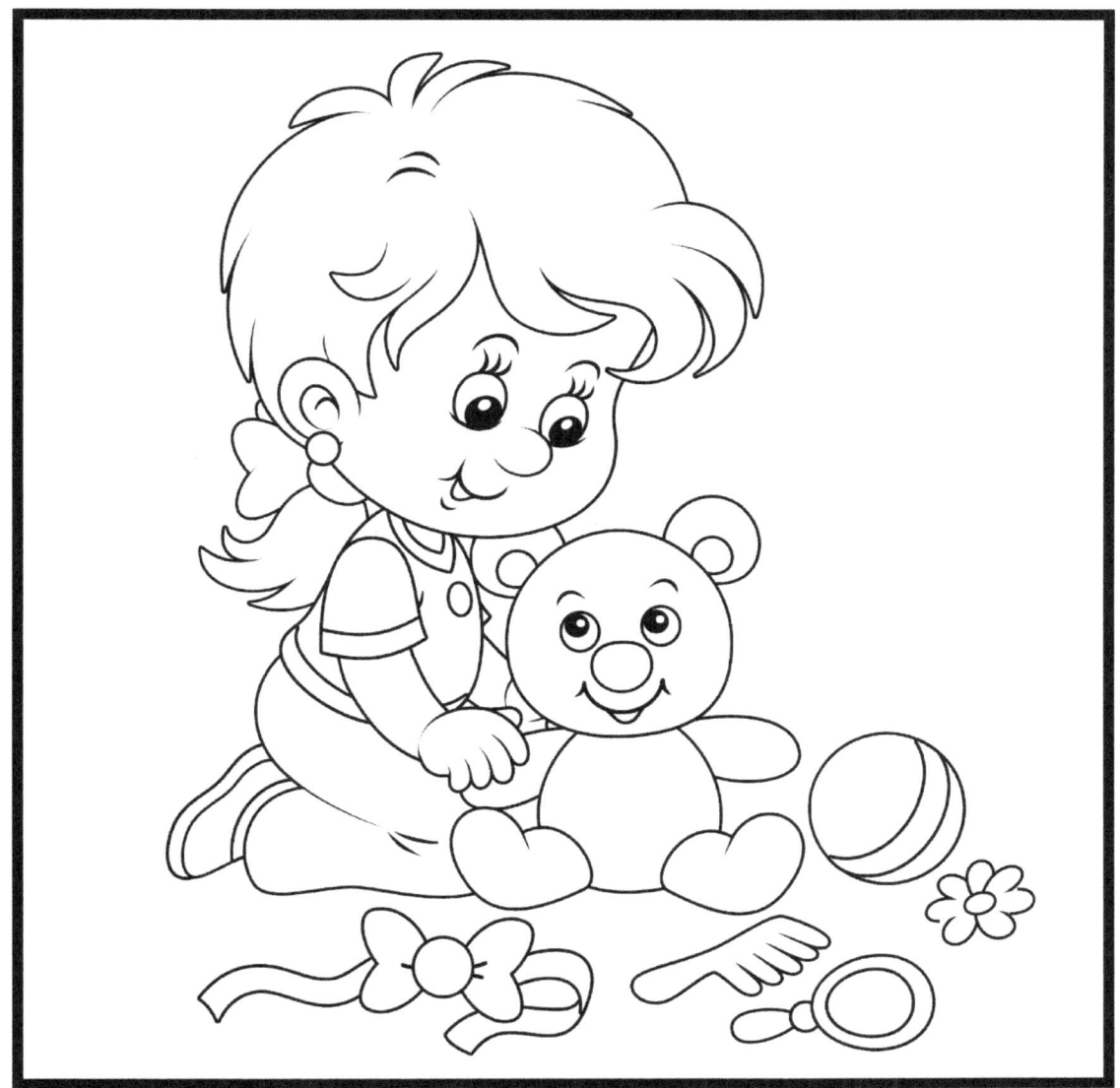

note:

_____

_____

_____

JANUARY 29TH

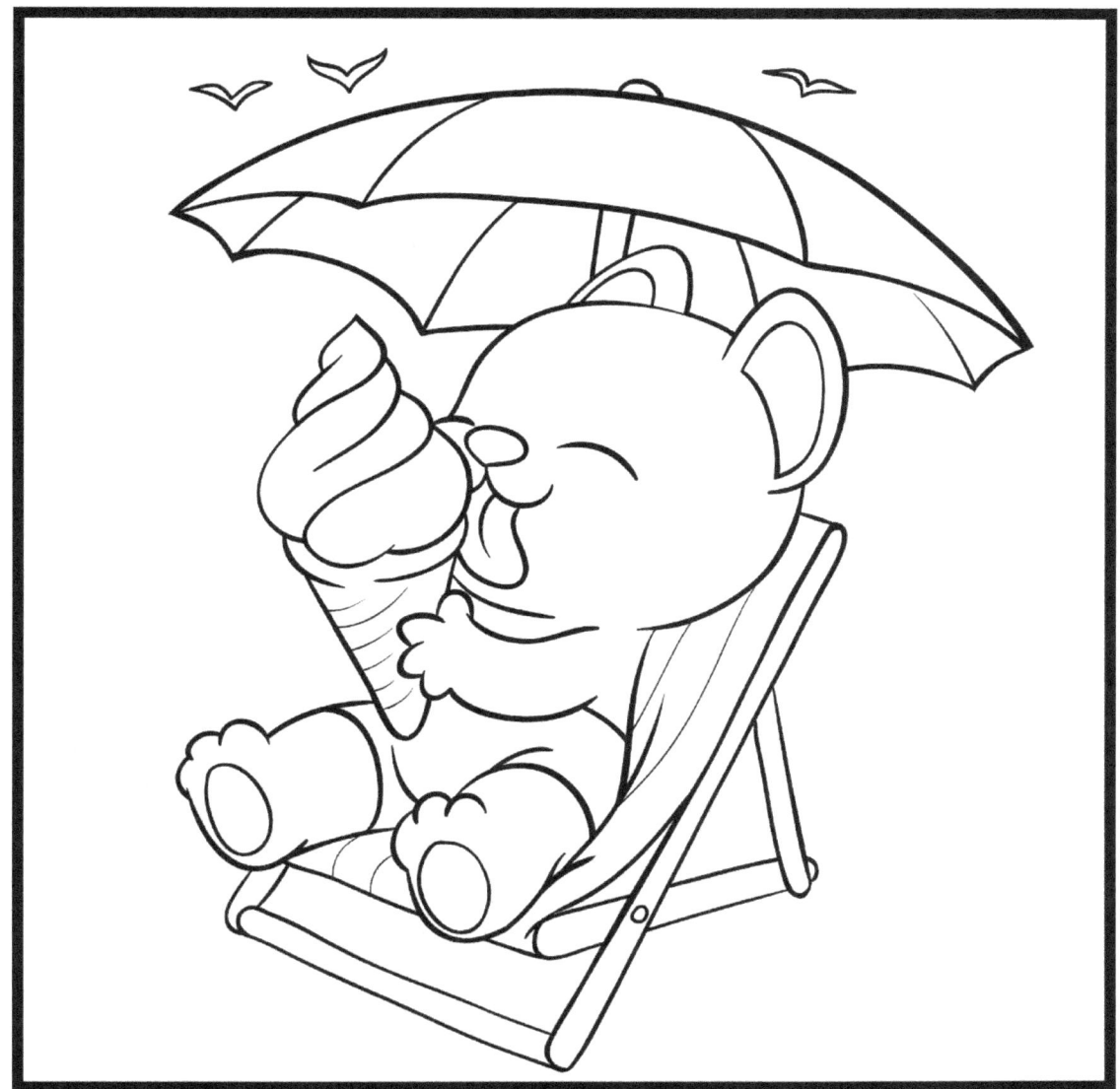

note:

_____

_____

_____

JANUARY 30TH

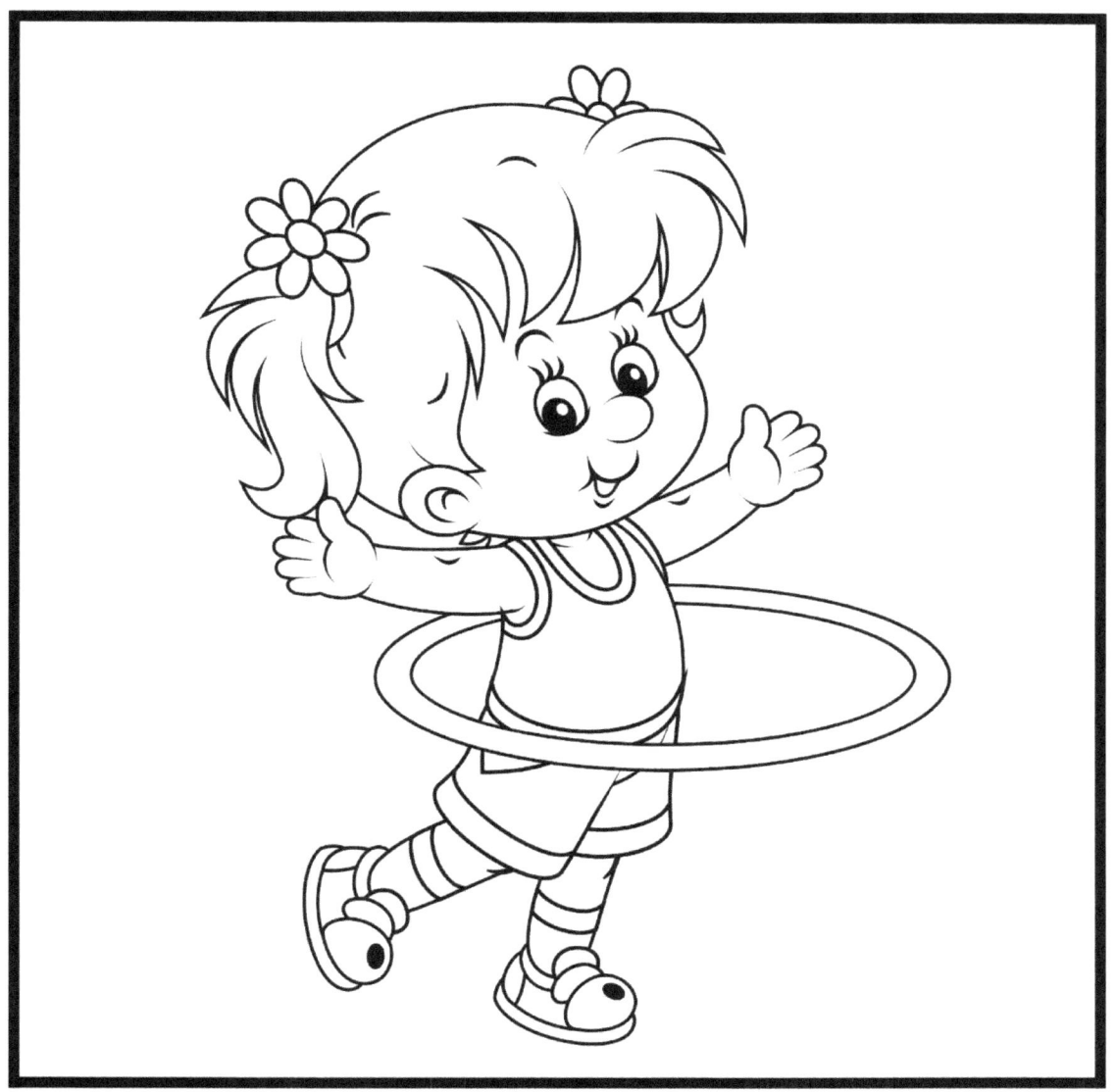

note:

_____

_____

_____

JANUARY 31TH

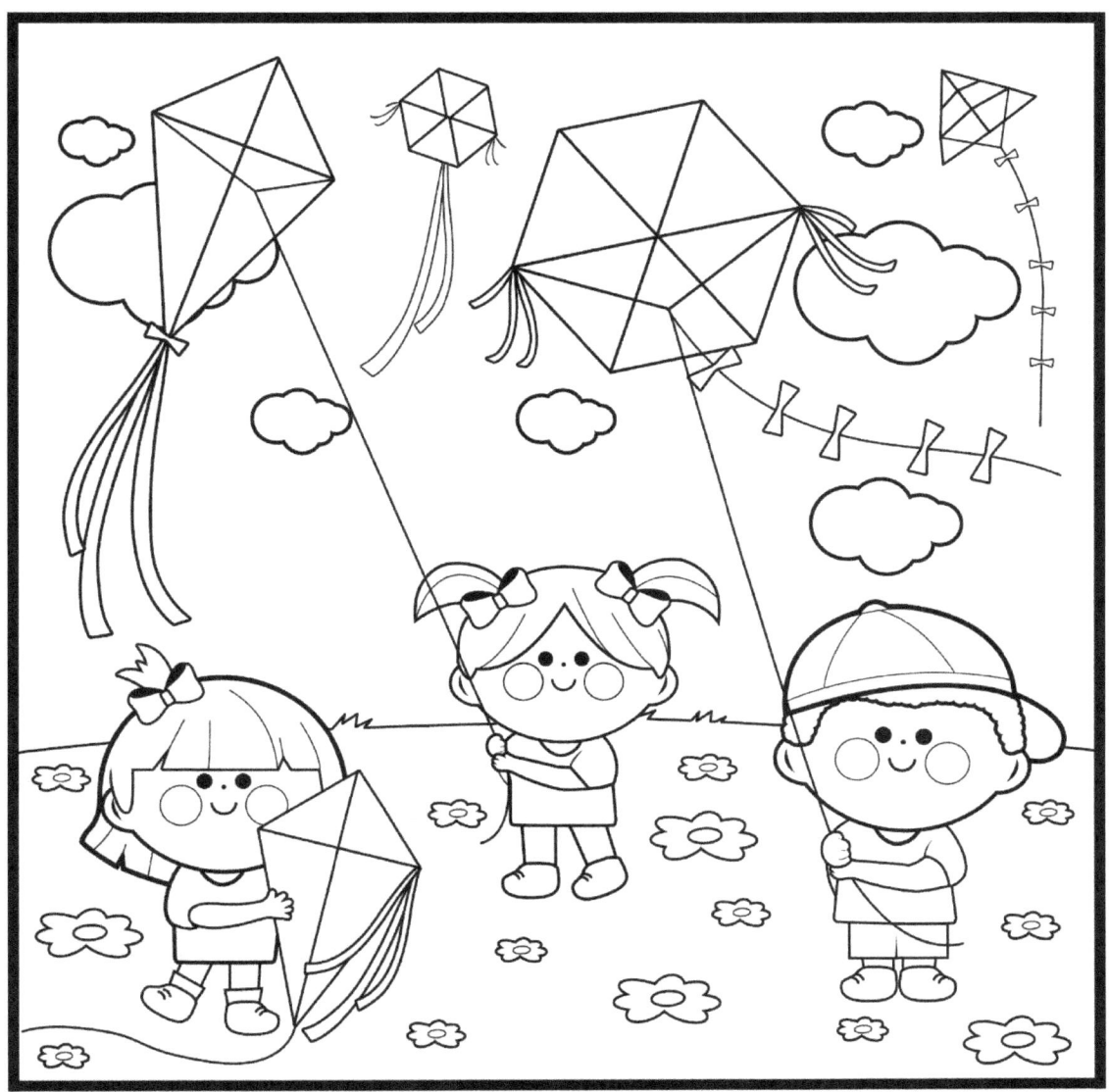

note:

_____

_____

_____

JANUARY 32TH

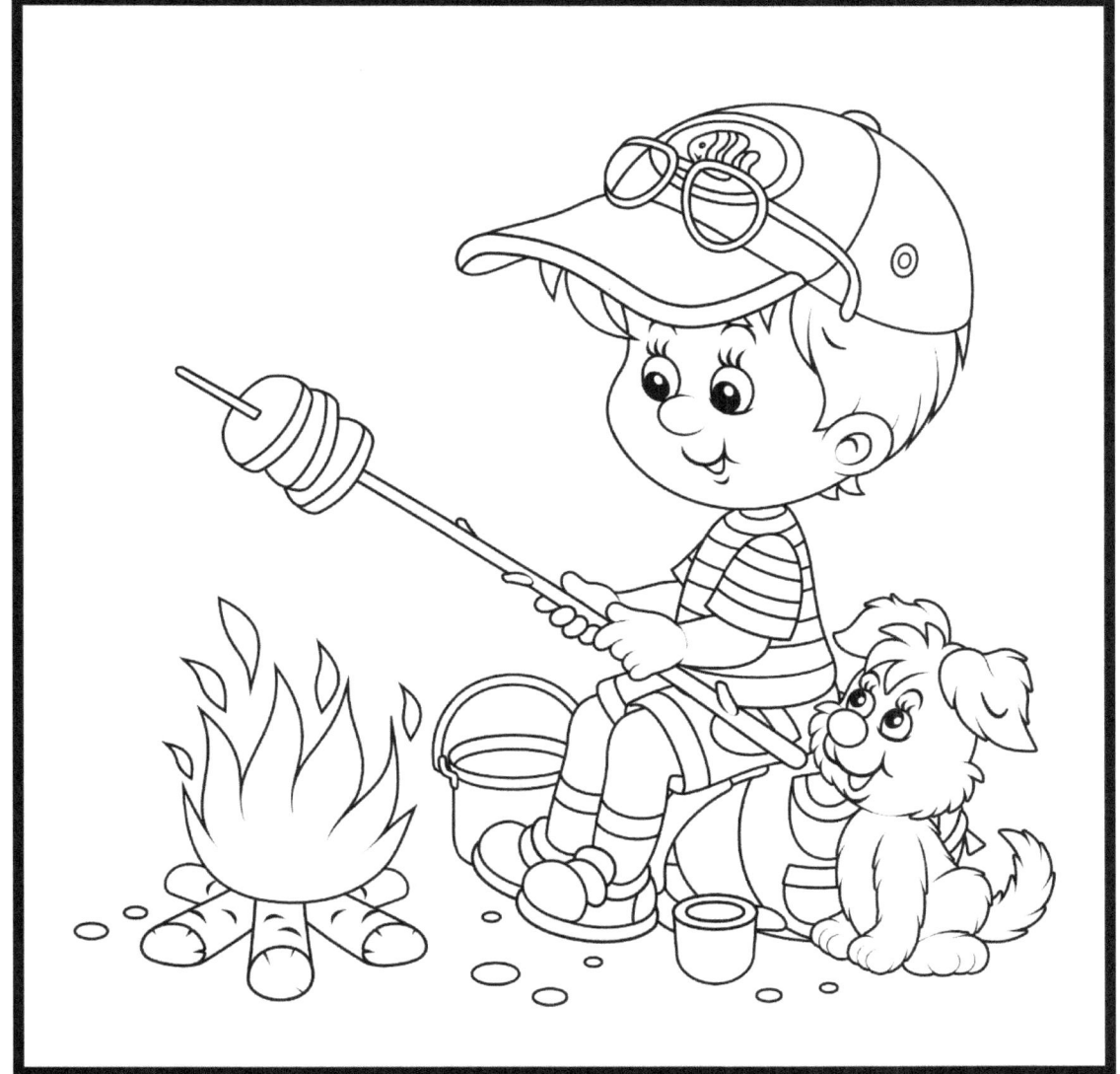

note:

_____

_____

_____

JANUARY 33TH

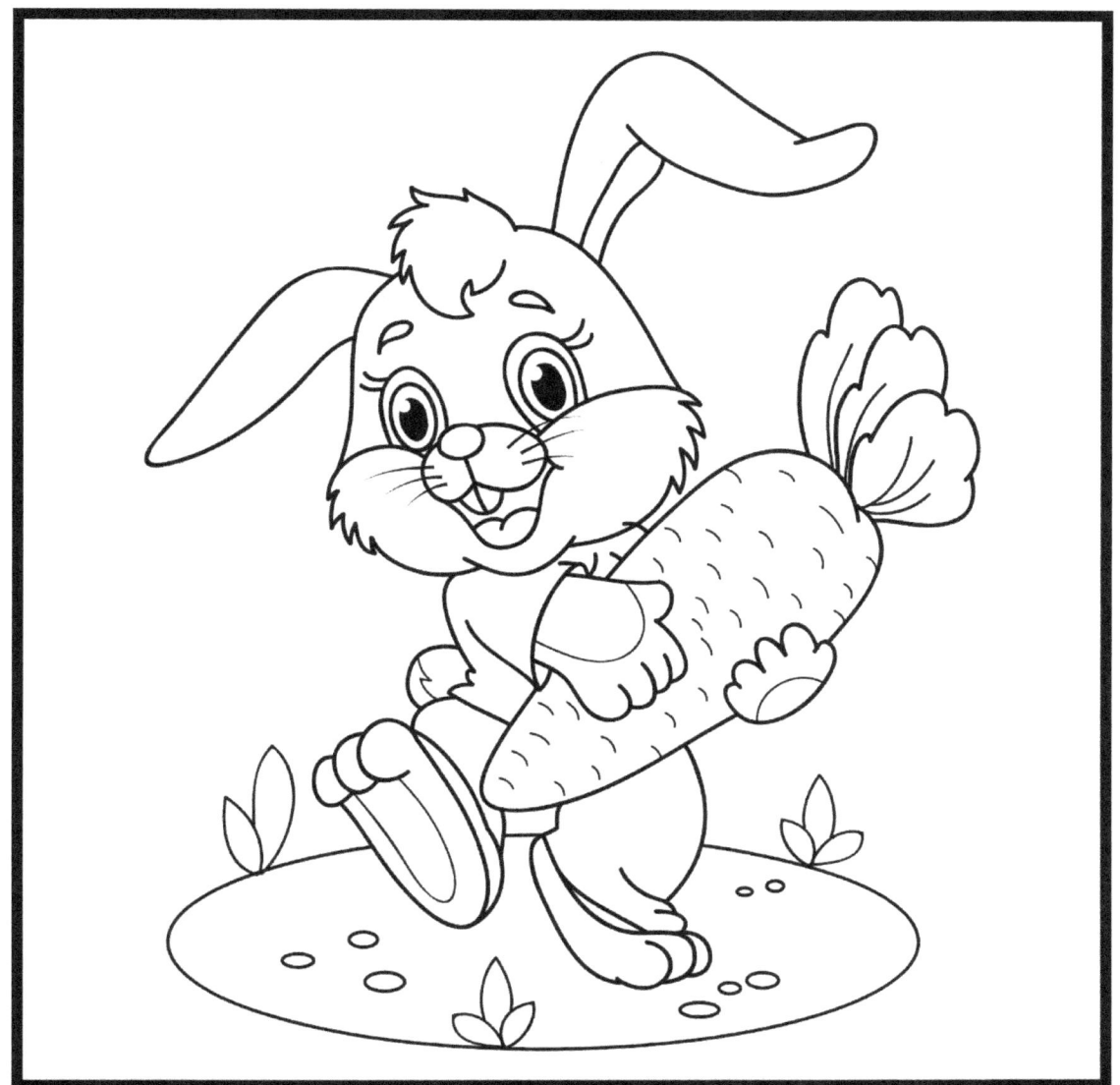

note:

_____

_____

_____

JANUARY 34TH

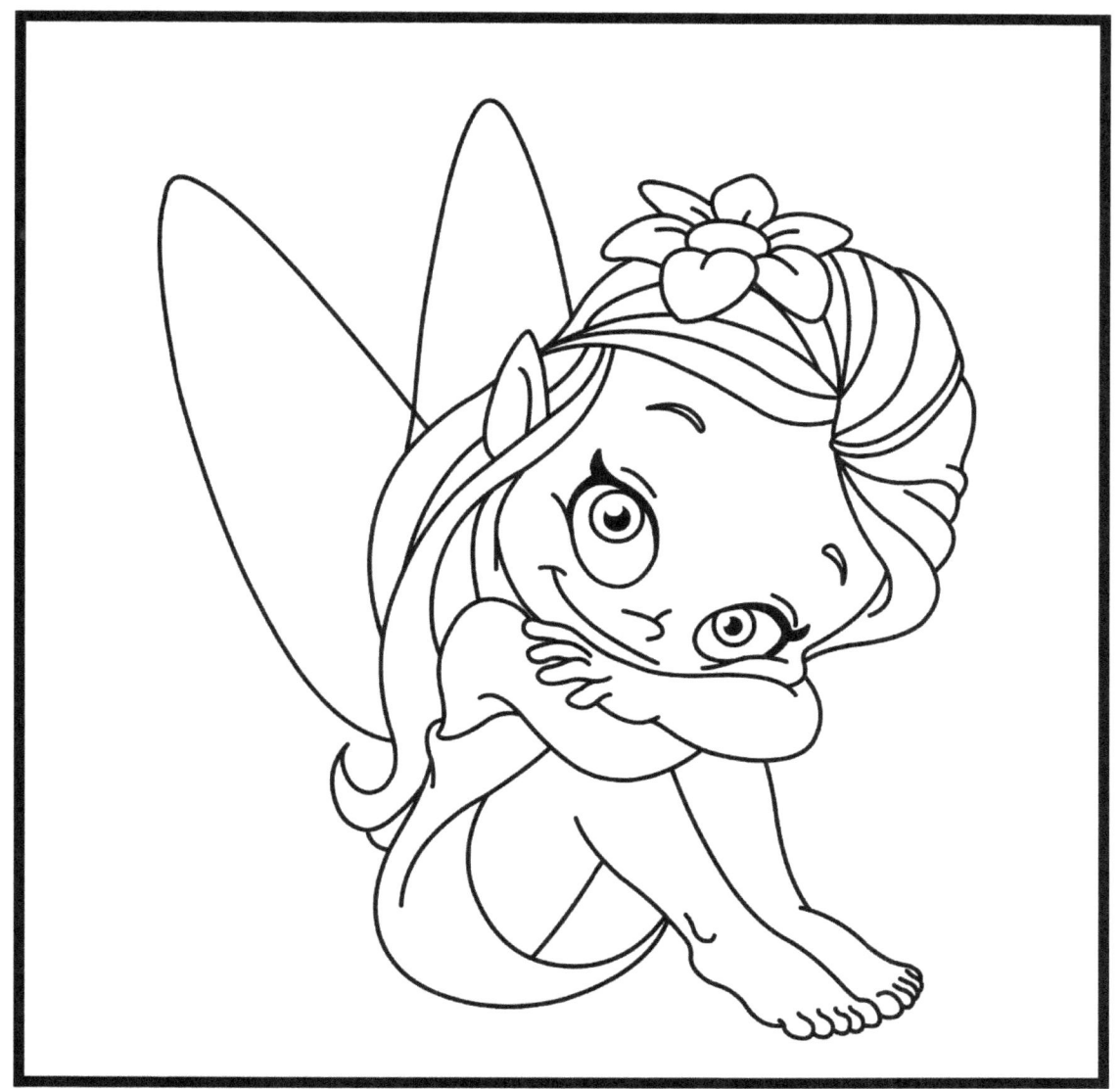

note:

_____

_____

_____

JANUARY 35TH

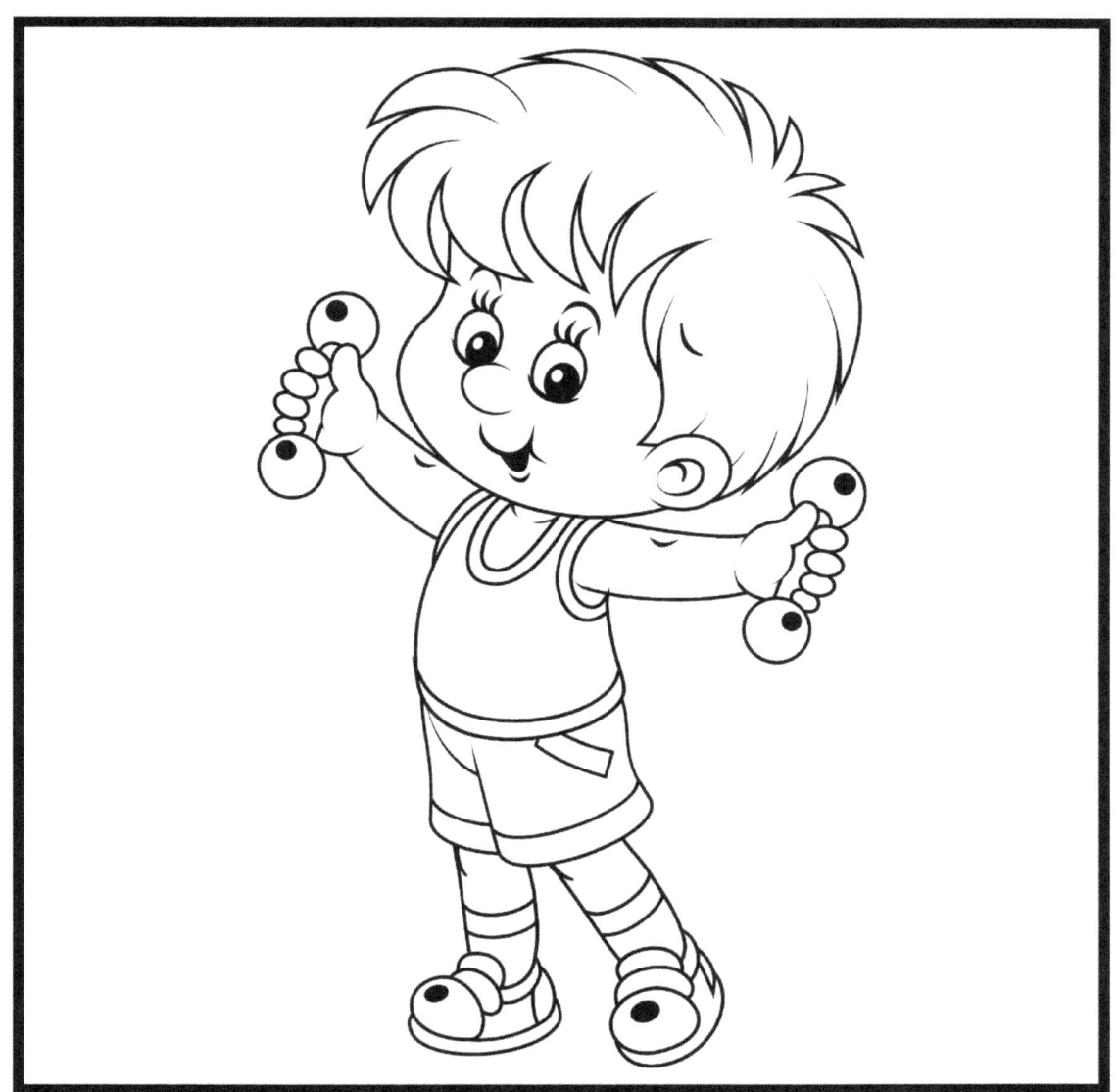

note:

_____

_____

_____

JANUARY 36TH

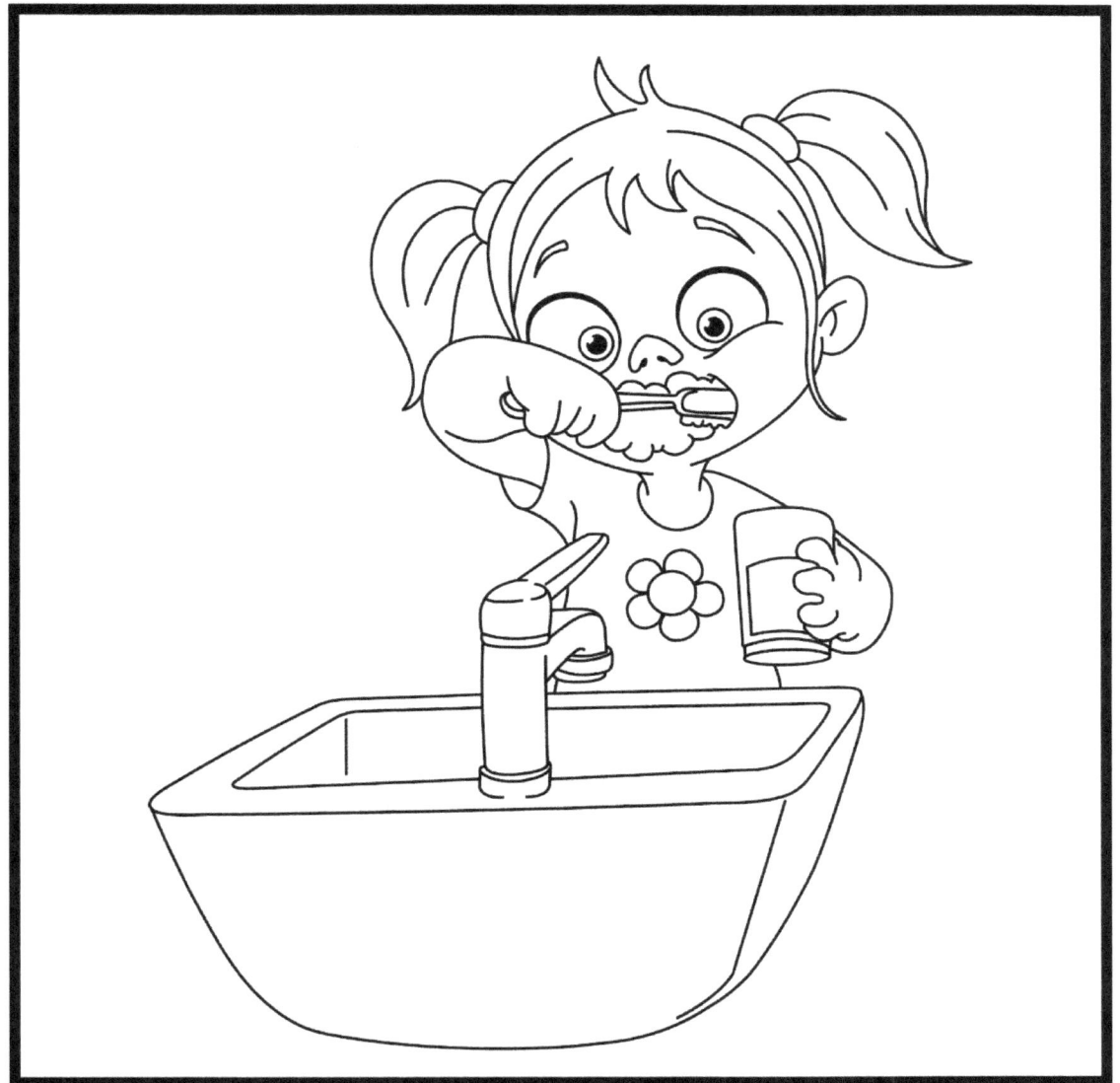

note:

_____

_____

_____

JANUARY 37TH

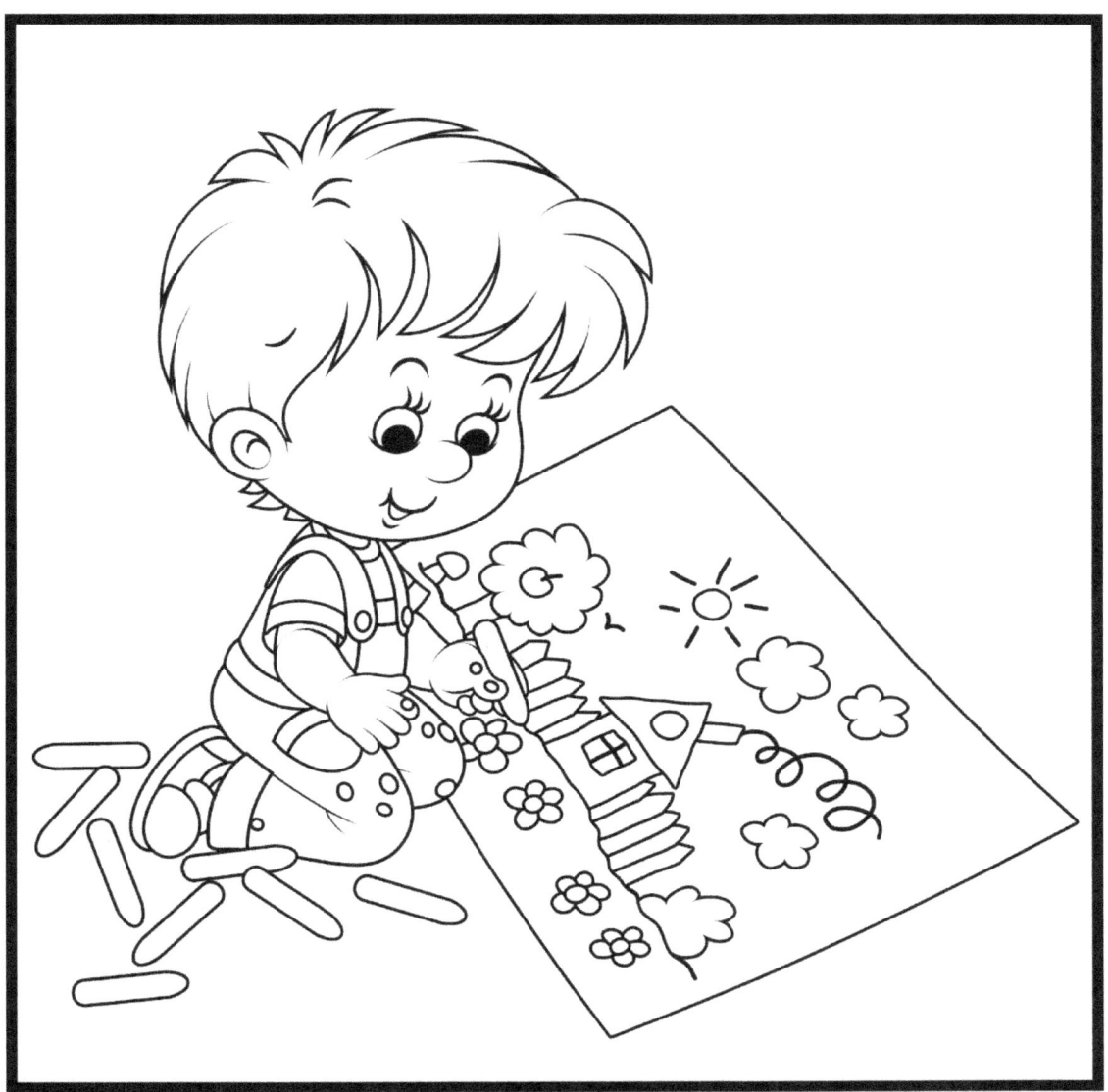

note:

_____

_____

_____

JANUARY 38TH

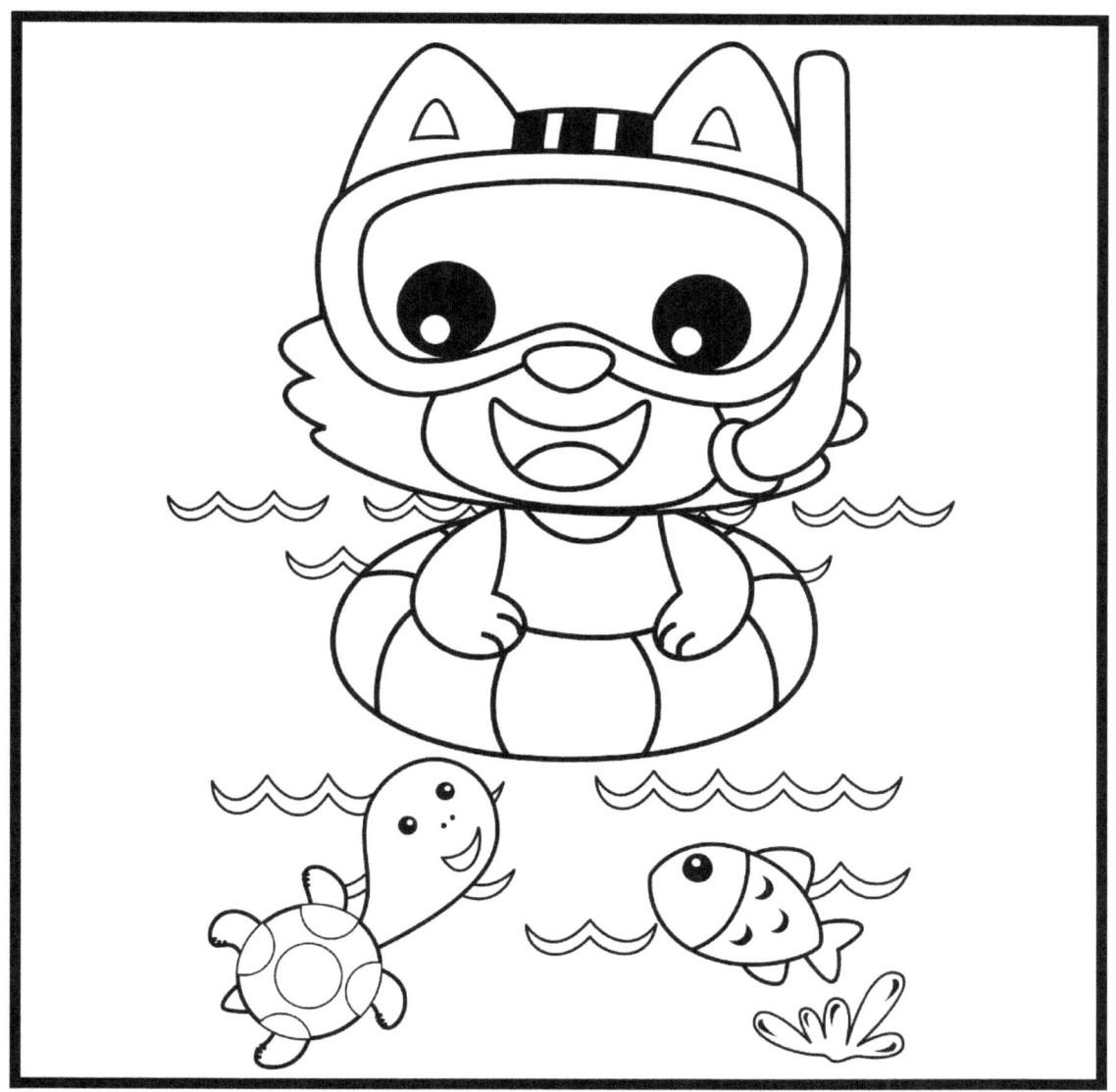

note:

_____

_____

_____

JANUARY 39TH

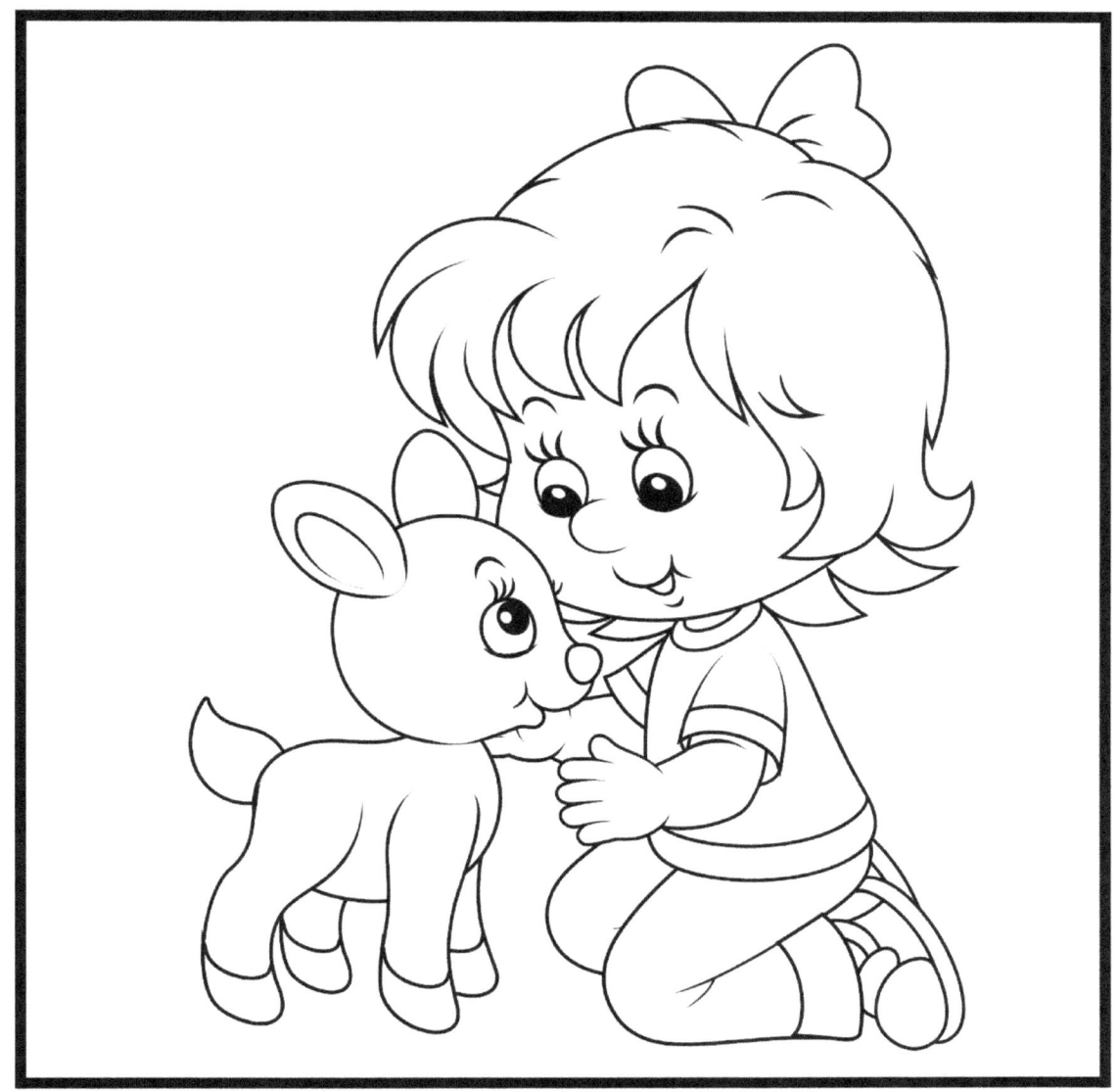

note:

_____

_____

_____

JANUARY 40TH

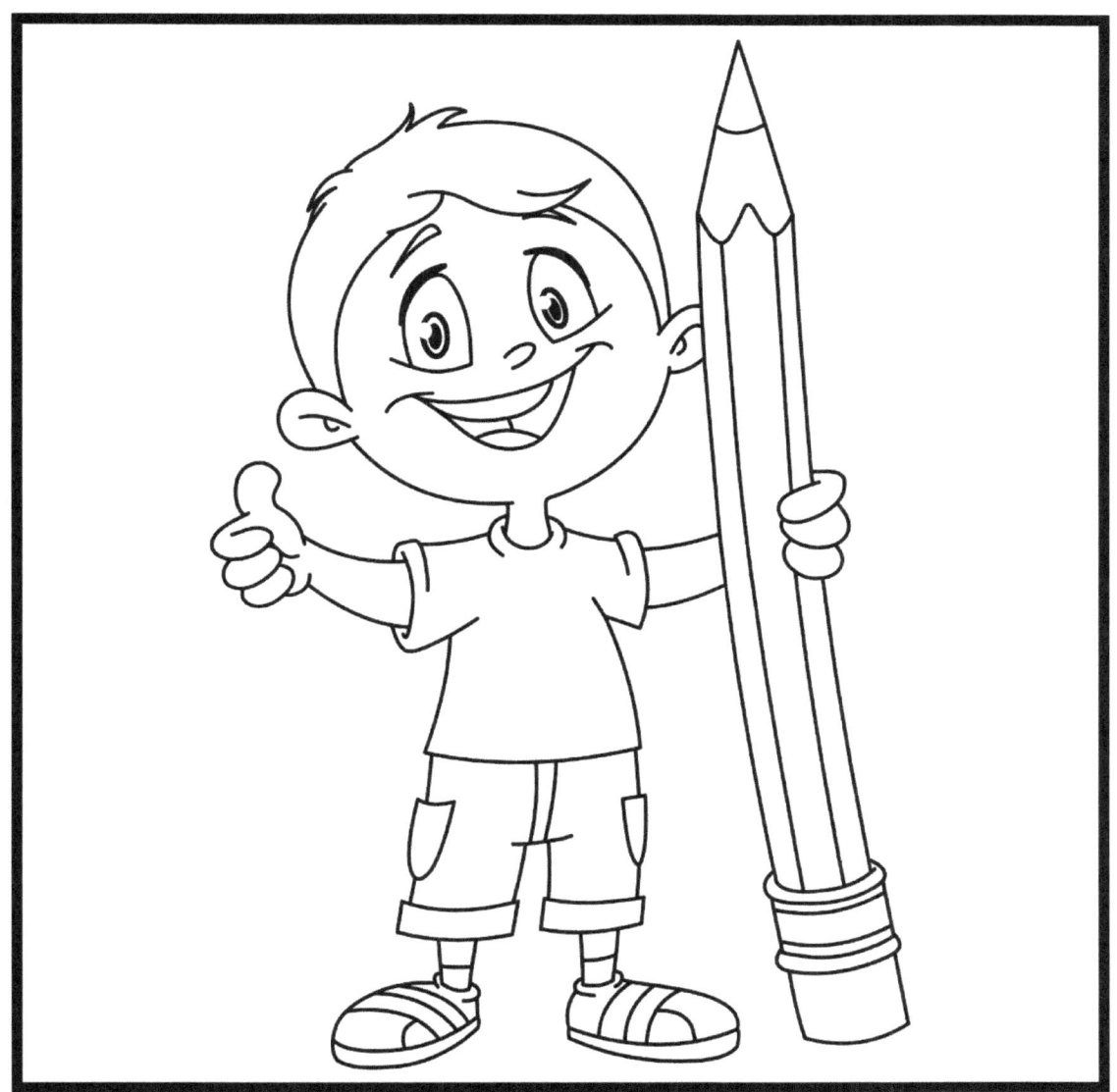

note:

_____

_____

_____

JANUARY 41TH

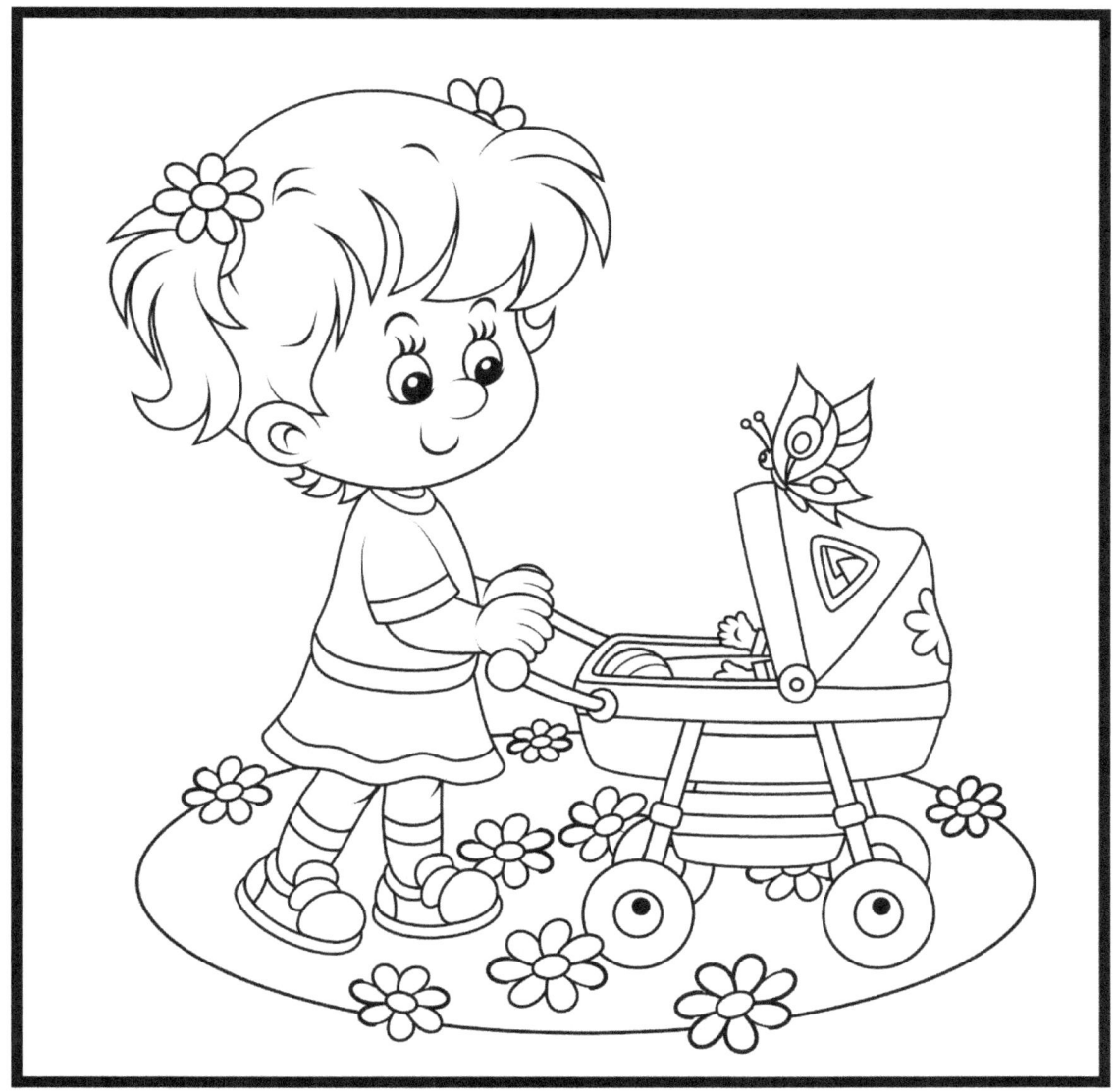

note:

_____

_____

_____

JANUARY 42TH

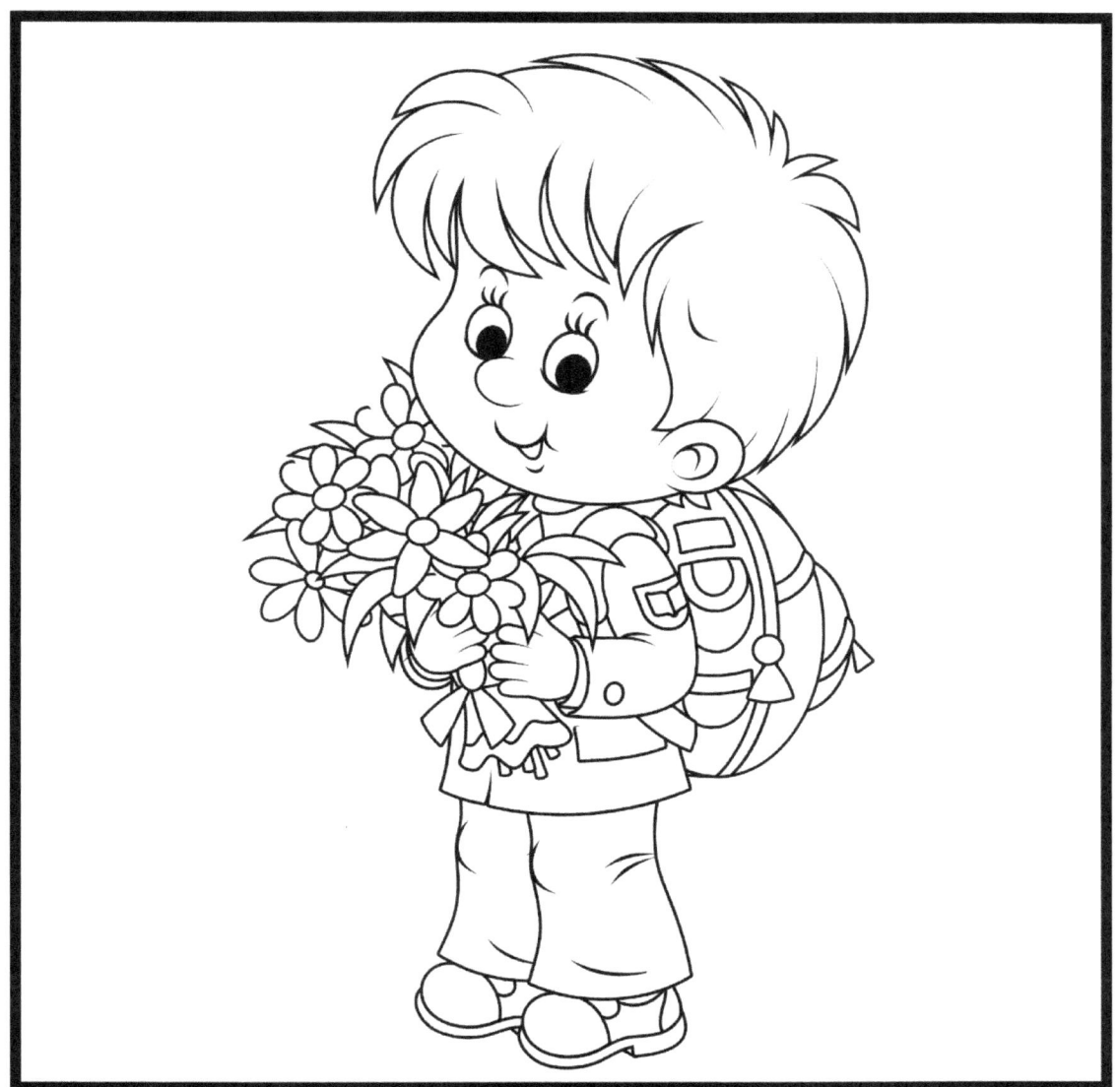

note:

_____

_____

_____

JANUARY 43TH

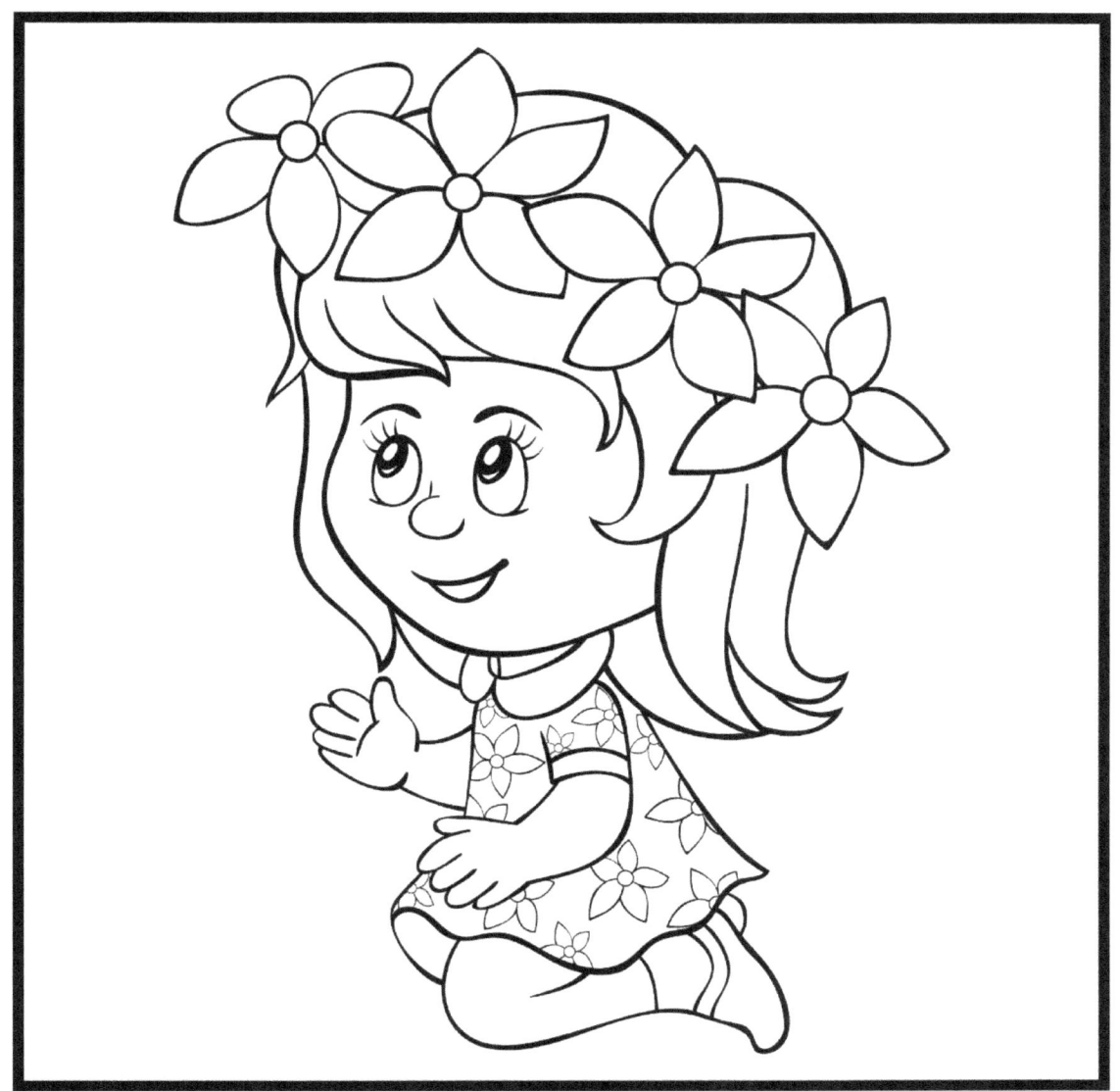

note:

_____

_____

_____

JANUARY 44TH

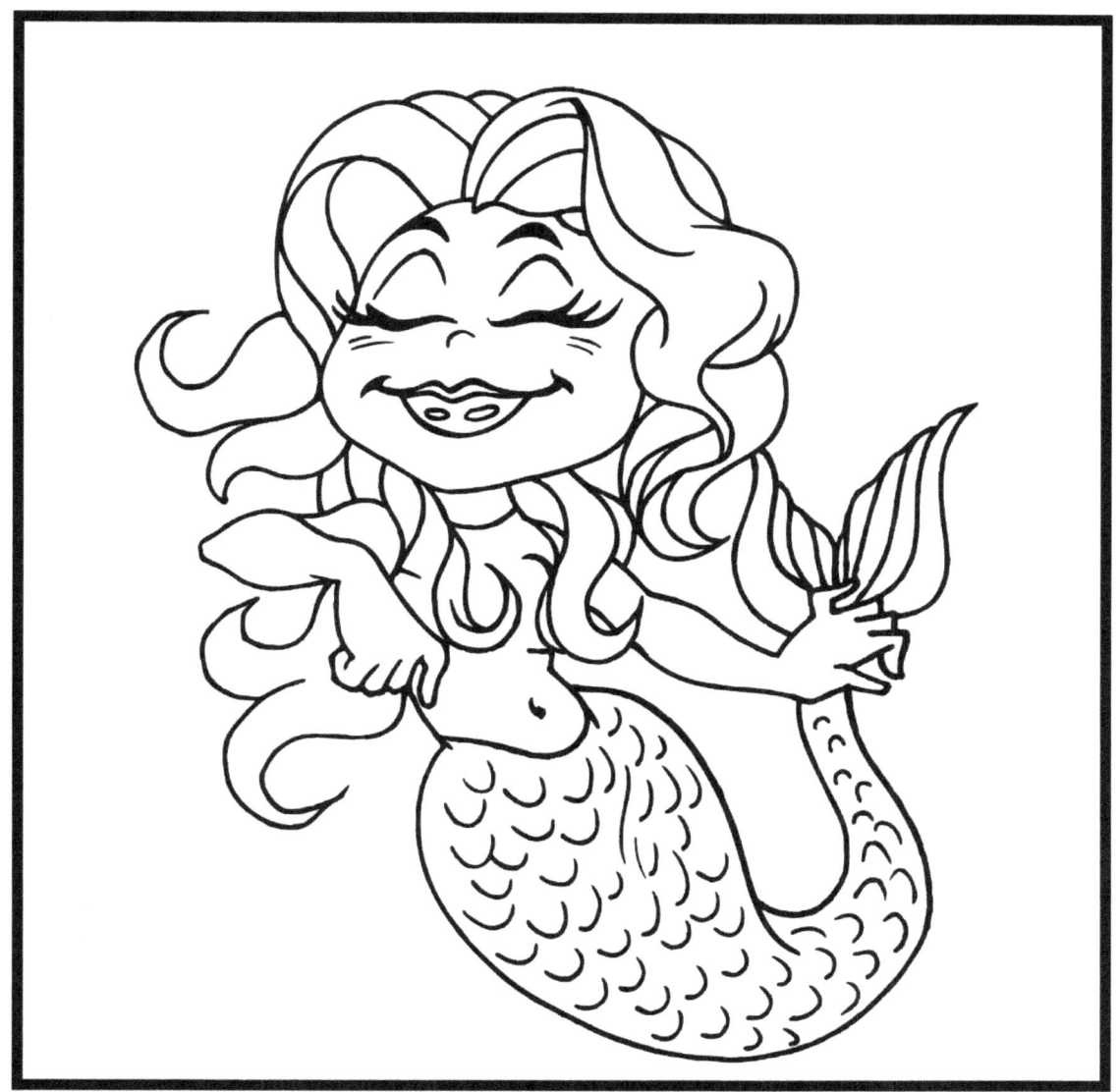

note:

_____

_____

_____

JANUARY 45TH

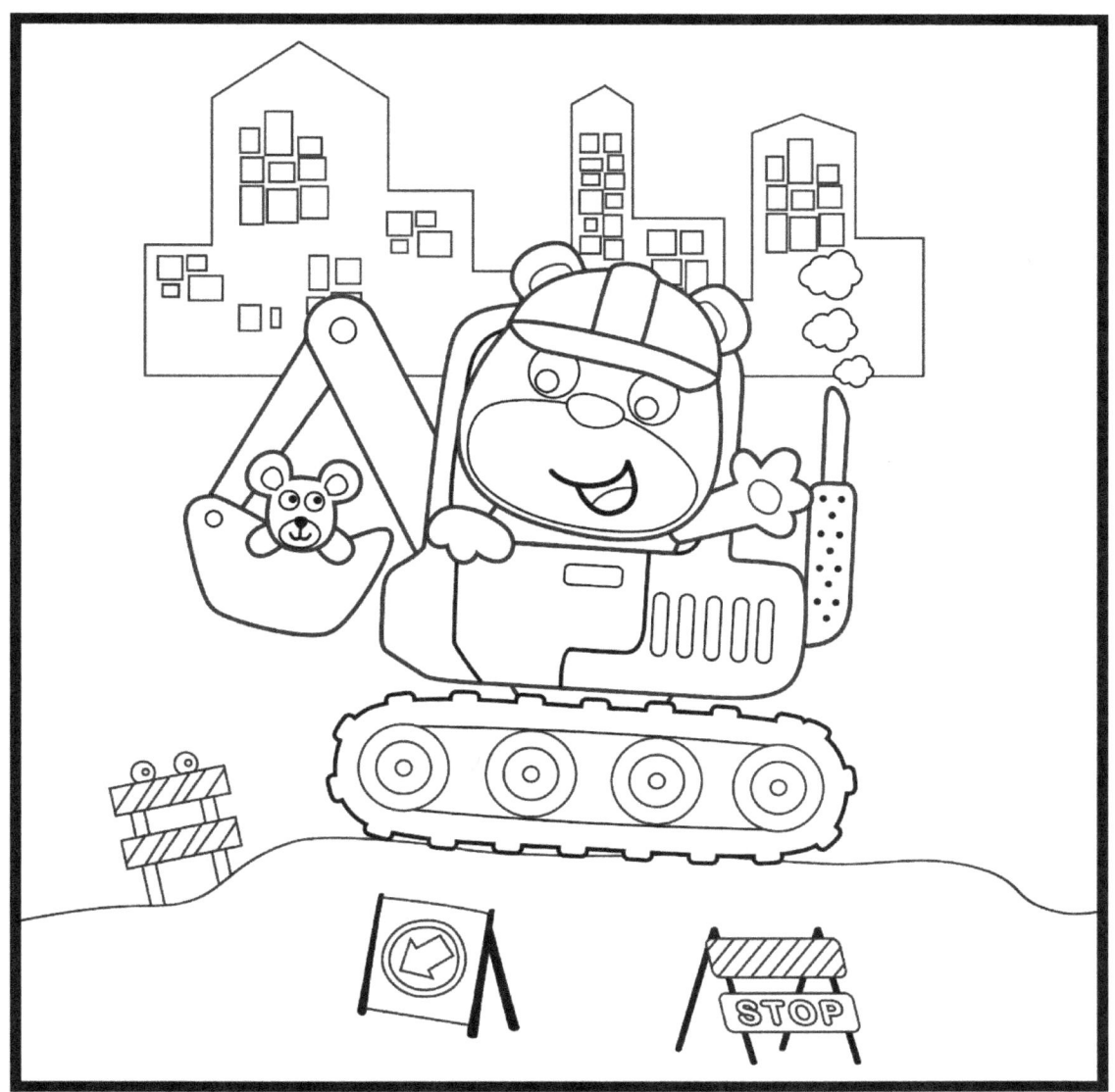

note:

_____

_____

_____

JANUARY 46TH

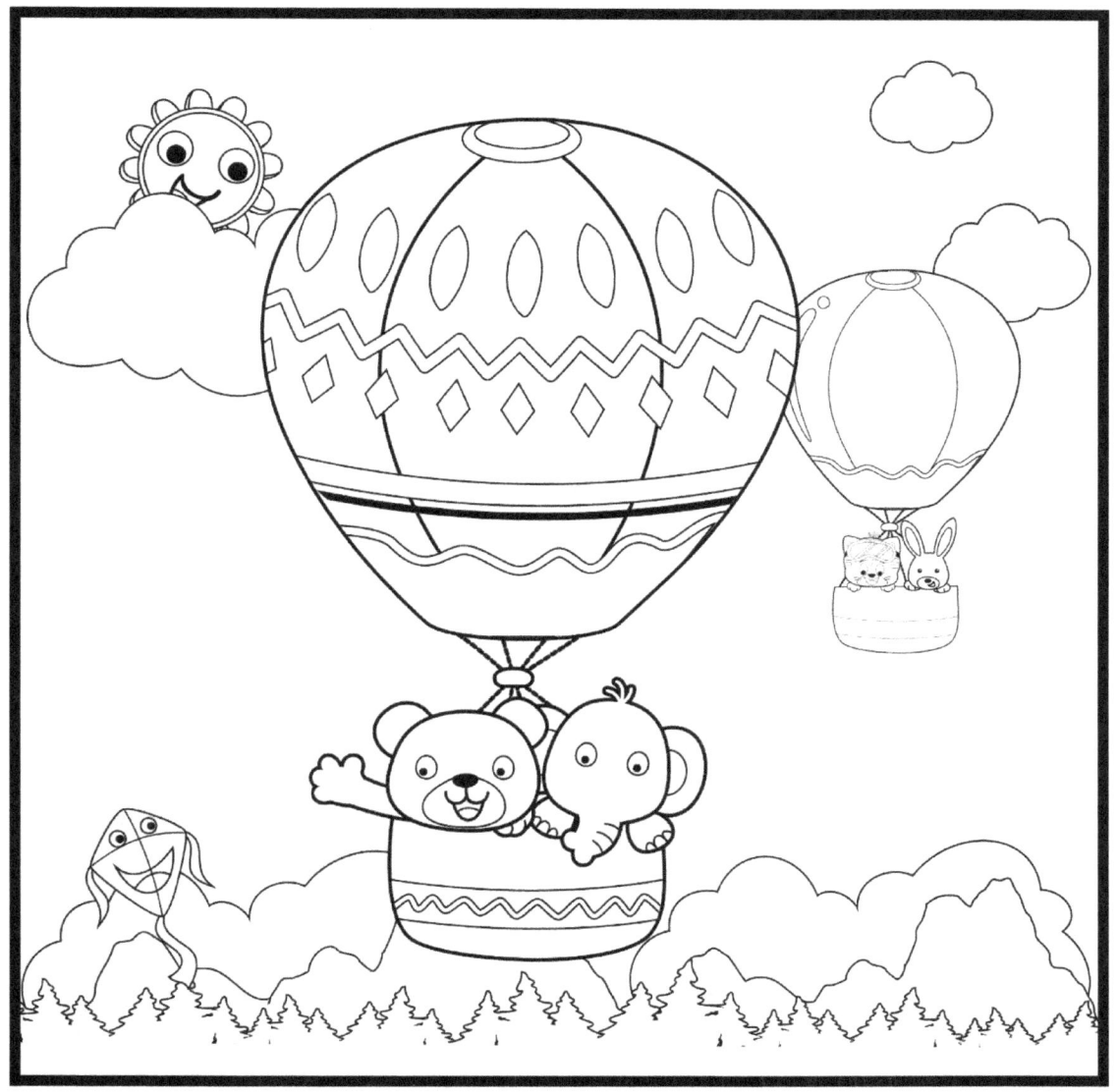

note:

_____

_____

_____

JANUARY 47TH

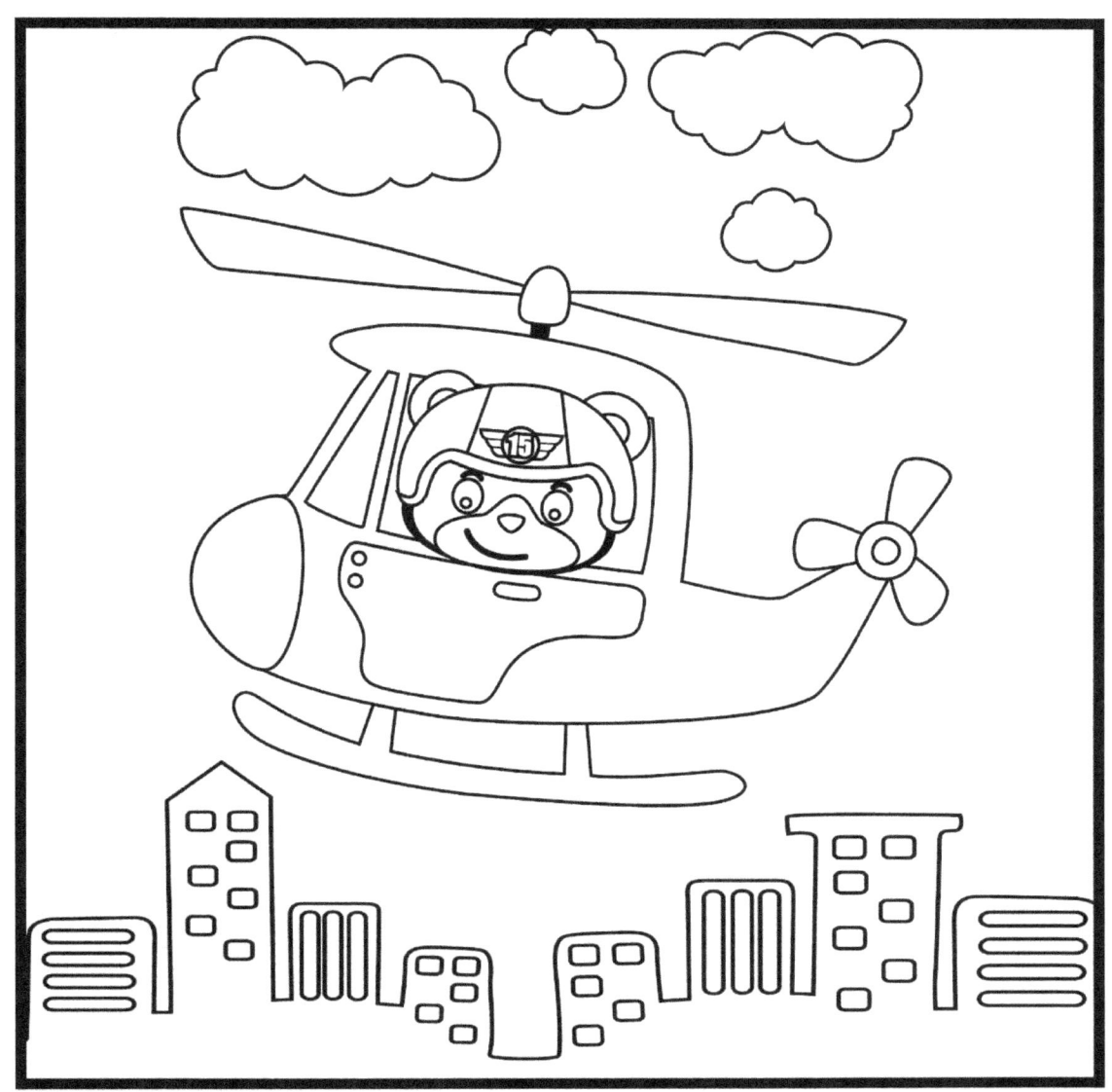

note:

_____

_____

_____

JANUARY 48TH

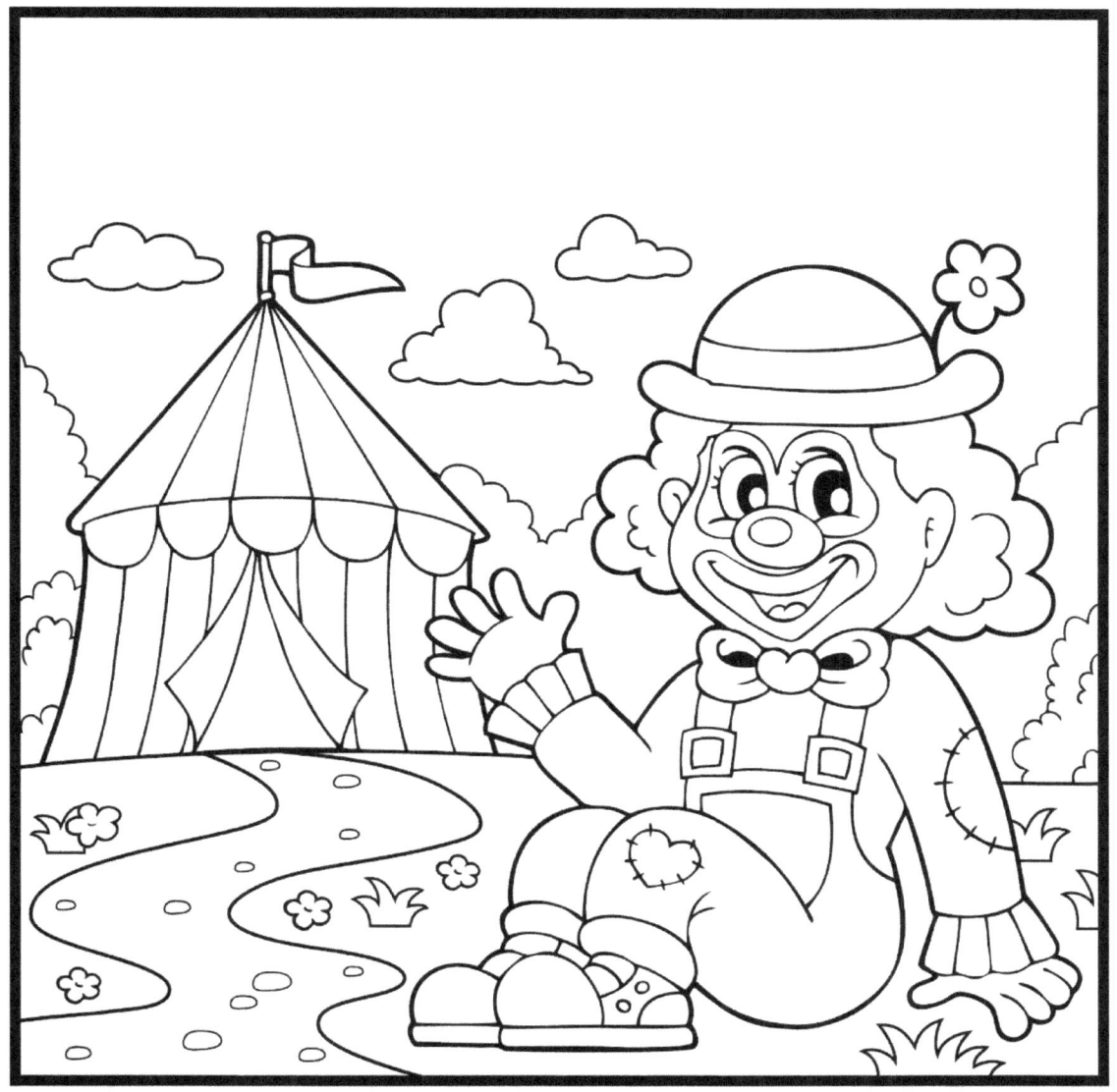

note:

_____

_____

_____

JANUARY 49TH

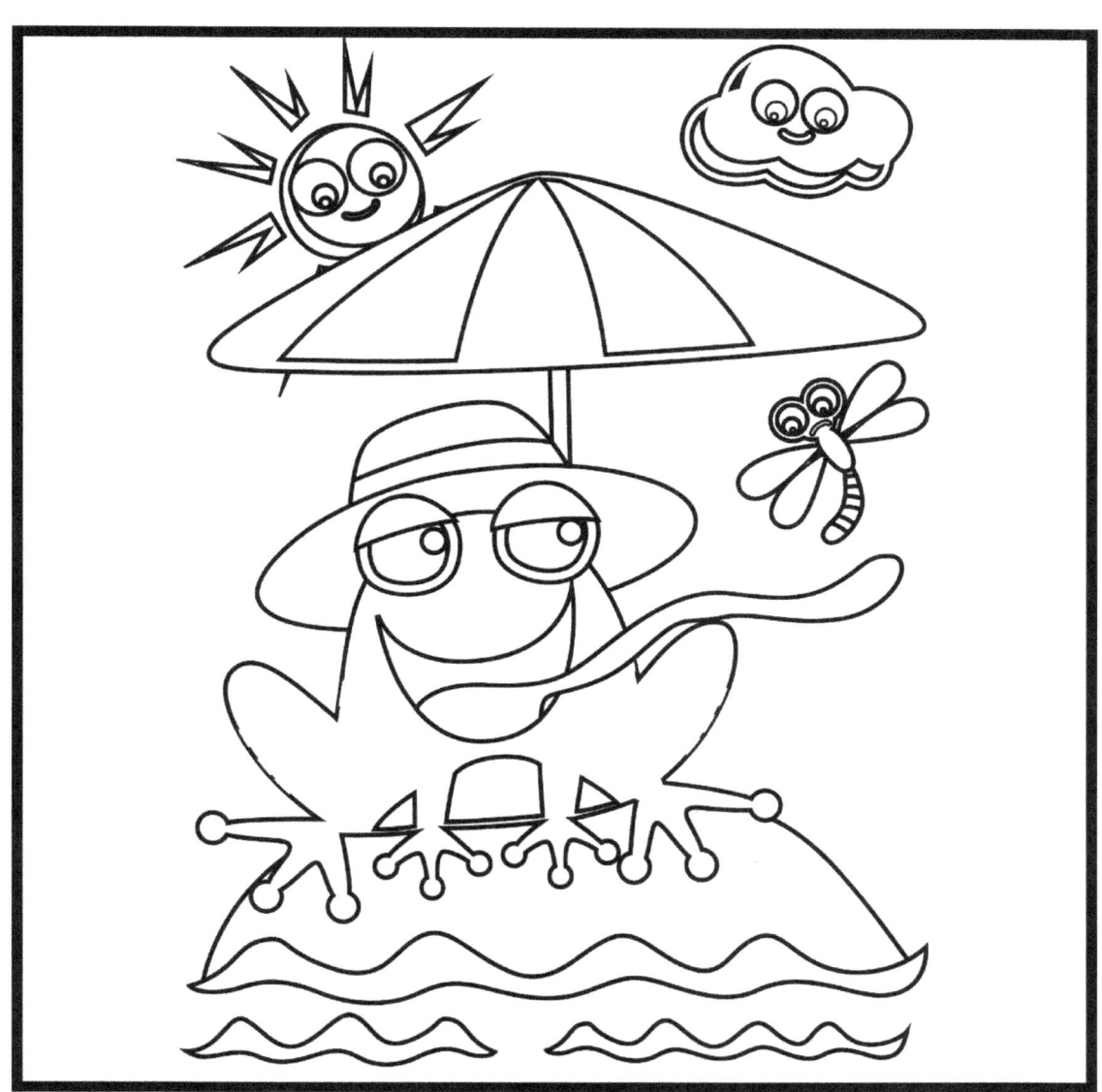

note:

_____

_____

_____

JANUARY 50TH

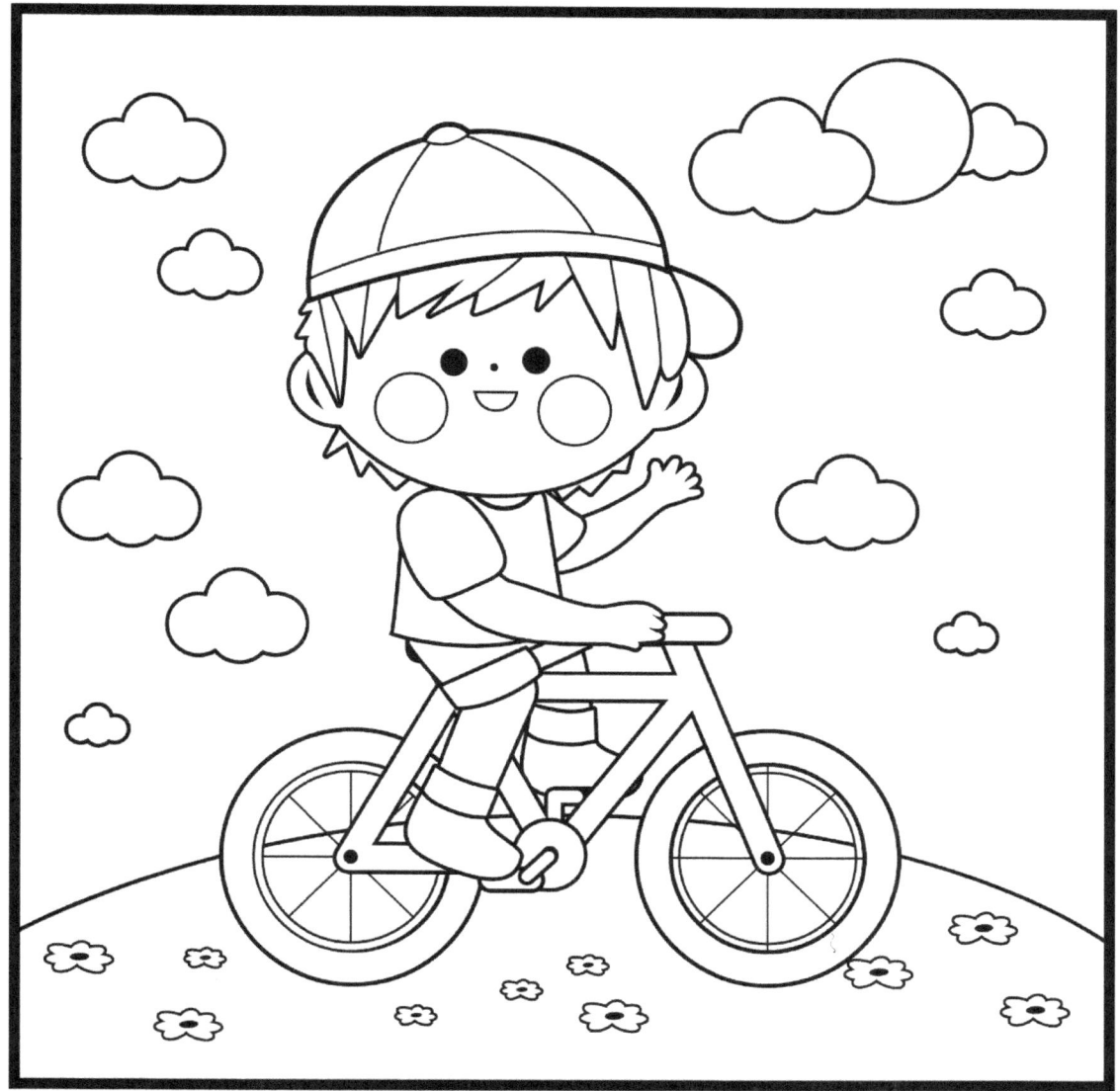

note:

_____

_____

_____

www.ingramcontent.com/pod-product-compliance
Lightning Source LLC
Chambersburg PA
CBHW081605220526
45468CB00010B/2779